Praise for *Extreme Programming Explained, Second Edition*

"In this second edition of *Extreme Programming Explained*, Kent Beck organizes and presents five years' worth of experiences, growth, and change revolving around XP. If you are seriously interested in understanding how you and your team can start down the path of improvement with XP, you must read this book."

—**Francesco Cirillo,** Chief Executive Officer, XPLabs S.R.L.

"The first edition of this book told us what XP was—it changed the way many of us think about software development. This second edition takes it farther and gives us a lot more of the 'why' of XP, the motivations and the principles behind the practices. This is great stuff. Armed with the 'what' and the 'why,' we can now all set out to confidently work on the 'how': how to run our projects better, and how to get agile techniques adopted in our organizations."

—**Dave Thomas,** The Pragmatic Programmers LLC

"This book is dynamite! It was revolutionary when it first appeared a few years ago, and this new edition is equally profound. For those who insist on cookbook checklists, there's an excellent chapter on 'primary practices,' but I urge you to begin by truly contemplating the meaning of the opening sentence in the first chapter of Kent Beck's book: 'XP is about social change.' You should do whatever it takes to ensure that every IT professional and every IT manager—all the way up to the CIO—has a copy of *Extreme Programming Explained* on his or her desk."

—**Ed Yourdon,** author and consultant

"XP is a powerful set of concepts for simplifying the process of software design, development, and testing. It is about minimalism and incrementalism, which are especially useful principles when tackling complex problems that require a balance of creativity and discipline."

—**Michael A. Cusumano,** Professor, MIT Sloan School of Management, and author of *The Business of Software*

"*Extreme Programming Explained* is the work of a talented and passionate craftsman. Kent Beck has brought together a compelling collection of ideas about programming and management that deserves your full attention. My only beef is that our profession has gotten to a point where such common-sense ideas are labeled 'extreme.' . . ."

—**Lou Mazzucchelli,** Fellow, Cutter Business Technology Council

"If your organization is ready for a change in the way it develops software, there's the slow incremental approach, fixing things one by one, or the fast track, jumping feet first into Extreme Programming. Do not be frightened by the name, it is not that extreme at all. It is mostly good old recipes and common sense, nicely integrated together, getting rid of all the fat that has accumulated over the years."

—**Philippe Kruchten,** UBC, Vancouver, British Columbia

"Sometimes revolutionaries get left behind as the movement they started takes on a life of its own. In this book, Kent Beck shows that he remains ahead of the curve, leading XP to its next level. Incorporating five years of feedback, this book takes a fresh look at what it takes to develop better software in less time and for less money. There are no silver bullets here, just a set of practical principles that, when used wisely, can lead to dramatic improvements in software development productivity."

—**Mary Poppendieck,** author of *Lean Software Development: An Agile Toolkit*

"Kent Beck has revised his classic book based on five more years of applying and teaching XP. He shows how the path to XP is both easy and hard: It can be started with fewer practices, and yet it challenges teams to go farther than ever."

—**William Wake,** independent consultant

"With new insights, wisdom from experience and clearer explanations of the art of Extreme Programming, this edition of Beck's classic will help many realize the dream of outstanding software development."

—**Joshua Kerievsky,** author, *Refactoring to Patterns,* and Founder, Industrial Logic, Inc.

"XP has changed the way our industry thinks about software development. Its brilliant simplicity, focused execution, and insistence on fact-based planning over speculation have set a new standard for software delivery."

—**David Trowbridge,** Architect, Microsoft Corporation

Extreme Programming Explained

Second Edition

The XP Series

Kent Beck, Series Advisor

Extreme Programming, familiarly known as XP, is a discipline of the business of software development that focuses the whole team on common, reachable goals. Using the values and principles of XP, teams apply appropriate XP practices in their own context. XP practices are chosen for their encouragement of human creativity and their acceptance of human frailty. XP teams produce quality software at a sustainable pace.

One of the goals of XP is to bring accountability and transparency to software development, to run software development like any other business activity. Another goal is to achieve outstanding results—more effective and efficient development with far fewer defects than is currently expected. Finally, XP aims to achieve these goals by celebrating and serving the human needs of everyone touched by software development—sponsors, managers, testers, users, and programmers.

The XP series exists to explore the myriad variations in applying XP. While XP began as a methodology addressing small teams working on internal projects, teams worldwide have used XP for shrink-wrap, embedded, and large-scale projects as well. The books in the series describe how XP applies in these and other situations, addressing both technical and social concerns.

Change has come to software development. However, change can be seen as an opportunity, not a threat. With a plan for change, teams can harness this opportunity to their benefit. XP is one such plan for change.

Titles in the Series

Extreme Programming Applied: Playing to Win, Ken Auer and Roy Miller

Extreme Programming Explained, Second Edition: Embrace Change, Kent Beck with Cynthia Andres

Extreme Programming Explored, William C. Wake

Extreme Programming for Web Projects, Doug Wallace, Isobel Raggett, and Joel Aufgang

Extreme Programming Installed, Ron Jeffries, Ann Anderson, and Chet Hendrickson

Planning Extreme Programming, Kent Beck and Martin Fowler

Testing Extreme Programming, Lisa Crispin and Tip House

Extreme Programming Explained

Second Edition

Embrace Change

Kent Beck
with Cynthia Andres

Addison-Wesley

Boston

Publisher: John Wait
Editor in Chief: Don O'Hagan
Acquisitions Editor: Paul Petralia
Managing Editor: John Fuller
Project Editors: Julie Nahil and Kim Arney Mulcahy
Compositor: Kim Arney Mulcahy
Manufacturing Buyer: Carol Melville

The publisher offers excellent discounts on this book when ordered in quantity for bulk purchases or special sales, which may include electronic versions and/or custom covers and content particular to your business, training goals, marketing focus, and branding interests. For more information, please contact:

U. S. Corporate and Government Sales
(800) 382-3419
corpsales@pearsontechgroup.com

For sales outside the U. S., please contact:

International Sales
international@pearsoned.com

Visit us on the Web: www.awprofessional.com

Library of Congress Cataloging-in-Publication Data

Beck, Kent.
    extreme programming explained: embrace change / Kent Beck with Cynthia Andres. — 2nd ed.
        p. cm.
    Includes bibliographical references and index.
    ISBN 0-321-27865-8 (alk. paper)
    1. Computer software—Development. 2. eXtreme programming. I. Title.
    QA76.76.D47B434 2004
    005.1—dc22

                                                        2004057463

ISBN 0-321-27865-8
Text printed in the United States on recycled paper at Courier in Stoughton, Massachusetts.

Second printing, February 2005

To Cindee

Without you, this book would still be about programmers hiding in a corner. Without you, I would still be one of those programmers.

Note To Programmers

Even programmers can be whole people in the real world. XP is an opportunity to test yourself, to be yourself, to realize that maybe you've been fine all along and just hanging with the wrong crowd.

Contents

Foreword to the Second Edition xv

Foreword to the First Edition xvii

Preface xxi

Chapter 1 *What is XP?* 1

Section 1 **Exploring XP** 9

Chapter 2 *Learning to Drive* 11

Chapter 3 *Values, Principles, and Practices* 13

Chapter 4 *Values* 17

    Communication 18

    Simplicity 18

    Feedback 19

    Courage 20

    Respect 21

    Others 21

Chapter 5 *Principles* 23

    Humanity 24

    Economics 25

    Mutual Benefit 26

Self-Similarity 27
Improvement 28
Diversity 29
Reflection 29
Flow 30
Opportunity 30
Redundancy 31
Failure 32
Quality 32
Baby Steps 33
Accepted Responsibility 34

Chapter 6   *Practices* 35

Chapter 7   *Primary Practices* 37
Sit Together 37
Whole Team 38
Informative Workspace 39
Energized Work 41
Pair Programming 42
Stories 44
Weekly Cycle 46
Quarterly Cycle 47
Slack 48
Ten-Minute Build 49
Continuous Integration 49
Test-First Programming 50
Incremental Design 51

Chapter 8   *Getting Started* 55

Chapter 9   *Corollary Practices* 61
Real Customer Involvement 61
Incremental Deployment 62
Team Continuity 63
Shrinking Teams 64
Root-Cause Analysis 64
Shared Code 66
Code and Tests 66
Single Code Base 67

Daily Deployment 68
Negotiated Scope Contract 69
Pay-Per-Use 69

Chapter 10 *The Whole XP Team* 73
Testers 74
Interaction Designers 75
Architects 75
Project Managers 76
Product Managers 77
Executives 78
Technical Writers 80
Users 81
Programmers 81
Human Resources 81
Roles 82

Chapter 11 *The Theory of Constraints* 85

Chapter 12 *Planning: Managing Scope* 91

Chapter 13 *Testing: Early, Often, and Automated* 97

Chapter 14 *Designing: The Value of Time* 103
Simplicity 109

Chapter 15 *Scaling XP* 111
Number of People 111
Investment 113
Size of Organization 113
Time 114
Problem Complexity 115
Solution Complexity 115
Consequences of Failure 116

Chapter 16 *Interview* 119

Section 2 **Philosophy of XP** 123

Chapter 17 *Creation Story* 125

Chapter 18 *Taylorism and Software* 131

Chapter 19 *Toyota Production System* 135

Chapter 20 *Applying XP* 139
Choosing a Coach 143
When You Shouldn't Use XP 144

Chapter 21 *Purity* 145
Certification and Accreditation 146

Chapter 22 *Offshore Development* 149

Chapter 23 *The Timeless Way of Programming* 153

Chapter 24 *Community and XP* 157

Chapter 25 *Conclusion* 159

Annotated Bibliography 161

Index 175

Foreword to the Second Edition

Wow—the second edition. I cannot believe that five years have already passed since the appearance of the first edition. When Kent pinged me to write a foreword to the second edition I asked him for a manuscript version with change bars. What a silly request—the book is a full rewrite! In the second edition of XP Explained Kent revisits XP and applies the XP paradigm—stay aware, adapt, change—to XP itself. Kent has revisited, cleaned-up, and refactored every bit of XP Explained and integrated many new insights. The result is XP Explained even better explained!

This is an excellent opportunity to reflect on how XP has influenced my own software development. Shortly after the first edition of XP Explained I became involved in the Eclipse project and it is now absorbing all my software energy. Eclipse isn't run under the pure XP flag. We follow agile practices; however, the XP influences are easy to spot. The most obvious one is that we have encoded several XP practices directly into our tool. Refactoring, unit testing, and immediate feedback as you code are now an integral part of our toolset. Moreover, since we are "eating our own dog food" we use these practices in our day-to-day development. Even more interesting are the XP influences one can spot in our development process. Eclipse is an open source project and one of our goals is to practice completely transparent development. The rationale is simple; if you don't know where the project is going you cannot help out or provide feedback. XP practices help us to achieve this goal.

Here is how we apply some of these practices:

✧ *Testing early, often and automated*—To get a green check mark for our latest builds more than 21,000 unit tests have to pass.

✧ *Incremental design*—We invest in the design every day, but we have the additional constraint that we need to keep our APIs stable.

✧ *Daily deployment*—Components deploy their code at least once per day and develop on top of the deployed code to get immediate feedback and to catch problems early.

✧ *Customer involvement*—We are lucky to have an active user community that isn't shy and provides us with continuous feedback. We listen and do our best to be responsive.

✧ *Continuous integration*—The latest code is built every night. The nightly builds provide us with insights about cross-component integration problems. Once per week we do an integration build where we ensure integrity across all components.

✧ *Short development cycles*—Our cycles are longer than the XP-suggested one week cycles, but the goals are the same. Each of our six week cycles ends in a milestone build which have become the heartbeat of our project. The goal of each milestone build is to show progress (which keeps us honest) and to deliver it with a high enough level of quality that our community can really use it and provide feedback (which keeps us even more honest).

✧ *Incremental planning*—After a release we develop an embryonic overall plan which we evolve throughout the release cycle. This plan is posted on our website early so that our user community can join the dialog. The exception is the milestones, which are fixed in the first planning iteration since they define the heartbeat of our project.

Despite the fact that we have not adopted XP in its entirety, we are getting a lot out of the above XP practices. In particular, they help us to reduce our development stress! All these practices, underpinned by a strong team committed to shipping quality software on time, are our keys to hitting the projected milestones and ship dates with precision.

Kent is continuing to challenge my views on software development. While reading the book I've discovered several practices that I will add to my try-list. I suggest you do the same and accept the XP invitation to improve the way you develop software and to create outstanding software.

Erich Gamma
September 2004

Foreword to
the First Edition

Extreme Programming (XP) nominates coding as the key activity throughout a software project. This can't possibly work!

Time to reflect for a second about my own development work. I work in a just-in-time software culture with compressed release cycles spiced up with high technical risk. Having to make change your friend is a survival skill. Communication in and across often geographically separated teams is done with code. We read code to understand new or evolving subsystem APIs. The life cycle and behavior of complex objects is defined in test cases, again in code. Problem reports come with test cases demonstrating the problem, once more in code. Finally, we continuously improve existing code with refactoring. Obviously our development is code-centric, but we successfully deliver software in time, so this can work after all.

It would be wrong to conclude that all that is needed to deliver software is daredevil programming. Delivering software is hard, and delivering quality software in time is even harder. To make it work requires the disciplined use of additional best practices. This is where Kent starts in his thought-provoking book on XP.

Kent was among the leaders at Tektronix to recognize the potential of man in the loop pair programming in Smalltalk for complex engineering applications. Together with Ward Cunningham, he inspired much of the pattern movement that has had such an impact on my career. XP describes an approach to development that combines practices used by many successful developers that got buried under the massive literature on software methods and process. Like patterns, XP builds on best practices such as unit testing, pair programming, and refactoring. In XP these practices are combined so that they complement and often control each other. The focus is on the interplay of the different practices, which makes this book an important contribution. There is a single goal to deliver software with the right functionality and hitting dates. While OTI's successful Just In Time Software process is not pure XP, it has many common threads.

I've enjoyed my interaction with Kent and practicing XP episodes on a little thing called JUnit. His views and approaches always challenge the way I approach software development. There is no doubt that XP challenges some traditional big M approaches; this book will let you decide whether you want to embrace XP or not.

Erich Gamma
August 1999

Preface

The goal of Extreme Programming (XP) is outstanding software development. Software can be developed at lower cost, with fewer defects, with higher productivity, and with much higher return on investment. The same teams that are struggling today can achieve these results by careful attention to and refinement of how they work, by pushing ordinary development practices to the extreme.

There are better ways and worse ways to develop software. Good teams are more alike than they are different. No matter how good or bad your team you can always improve. I intend this book as a resource for you as you try to improve.

This book is my personal take on what it is that good software development teams have in common. I've taken things I've done that have worked well and things I've seen done that worked well and distilled them to what I think is their purest, most "extreme" form. What I'm most struck with in this process is the limitations of my own imagination in this effort. Practices that seemed impossibly extreme five years ago, when the first edition of this book was published, are now common. Five years from now the practices in this book will probably seem conservative.

If I only talked about what good teams *do* I would be missing the point. There are legitimate differences between outstanding teams' actions based on the context in which they work. Looking below the surface, where their activities become ripples in the river hinting at shapes below, there is an intellectual and intuitive substrate to software development excellence that I have also tried to distill and document.

Critics of the first edition have complained that it tries to force them to program in a certain way. Aside from the absurdity of me being able to control anyone else's behavior, I'm embarrassed to say that was my intention. Relinquishing the illusion of control of other people's behavior and acknowledging each individual's responsibility for his or her own choices, in this edition I have tried to rephrase my message in a positive, inclusive way. I present proven practices you can add to your bag of tricks.

- ✧ No matter the circumstance you can always improve.
- ✧ You can always start improving with yourself.
- ✧ You can always start improving today.

Acknowledgments

I would like to thank my most excellent group of reviewers, each of whom spent considerable time reading and commenting on the manuscript: Francesco Cirillo, Steve McConnell, Mike Cohn, David Anderson, Joshua Kerievsky, Beth Andres-Beck, and Bill Wake. The Silicon Valley Patterns Group also provided valuable feedback on drafts: Chris Lopez, John Parello, Phil Goodwin, Dave Smith, Keith Ray, Russ Rufer, Mark Taylor, Sudarsan Piduri, Tracy Bialik, Jan Chong, Rituraj Kirti, Carlos Mc Evilly, Bill Venners, Wayne Vucenic, Raj Baskaran, Tim Huske, Patrick Manion, Jeffrey Miller, and Andrew Chase. Thanks to the production staff at Pearson: Julie Nahil, Kim Arney Mulcahy, and Michelle Vincenti. Paul Petralia, my editor, saw me through difficult times with humor and understanding. He taught me lessons in the value of relationships. Erich Gamma, my pair programming partner, provided conversation and feedback. The owners and staff of Bluestone Bakery and Cafe kept the hot chocolate and broadband flowing. Joëlle Andres-Beck edited copy and collected garbage. All of my children; Lincoln, Lindsey, Forrest, and Joëlle; spent many hours at Bluestone while we edited. Gunjan Doshi provided thought-provoking questions.

Finally, I cannot possibly give sufficient thanks to my wife, developmental editor, friend, and intellectual colleague Cynthia Andres.

Chapter 1

What is XP?

Extreme Programming (XP) is about social change. It is about letting go of habits and patterns that were adaptive in the past, but now get in the way of us doing our best work. It is about giving up the defenses that protect us but interfere with our productivity. It may leave us feeling exposed.

It is about being open about what we are capable of doing and then doing it. And, allowing and expecting others to do the same. It is about getting past our adolescent surety that "I know better than everyone else and all I need is to be left alone to be the greatest." It is about finding our adult place in the larger world, finding our place in the community including the realm of business/work. It is about the process of becoming more of our best selves and in the process our best as developers. And, it is about writing great code that is really good for business.

Good relationships lead to good business. Productivity and confidence are related to our human relationships in the workplace as well as to our coding or other work activities. You need both technique and good relationships to be successful. XP addresses both.

Prepare for success. Don't protect yourself from success by holding back. Do your best and then deal with the consequences. That's extreme. You leave yourself exposed. For some people that is incredibly scary, for others it's daily life. That is why there are such polarized reactions to XP.

XP is a style of software development focusing on excellent application of programming techniques, clear communication, and teamwork which allows us to accomplish things we previously could not even imagine. XP includes:

- A philosophy of software development based on the values of communication, feedback, simplicity, courage, and respect.
- A body of practices proven useful in improving software development. The practices complement each other, amplifying their effects. They are chosen as expressions of the values.
- A set of complementary principles, intellectual techniques for translating the values into practice, useful when there isn't a practice handy for your particular problem.
- A community that shares these values and many of the same practices.

XP is a path of improvement to excellence for people coming together to develop software. It is distinguished from other methodologies by:

- Its short development cycles, resulting in early, concrete, and continuing feedback.
- Its incremental planning approach, which quickly comes up with an overall plan that is expected to evolve through the life of the project.
- Its ability to flexibly schedule the implementation of functionality, responding to changing business needs.
- Its reliance on automated tests written by programmers, customers, and testers to monitor the progress of development, to allow the system to evolve, and to catch defects early.
- Its reliance on oral communication, tests, and source code to communicate system structure and intent.
- Its reliance on an evolutionary design process that lasts as long as the system lasts.
- Its reliance on the close collaboration of actively engaged individuals with ordinary talent.
- Its reliance on practices that work with both the short-term instincts of the team members and the long-term interests of the project.

The first edition of *Extreme Programming Explained: Embrace Change* had a definition of XP with the advantage of clarity: "XP is a lightweight methodology for small-to-medium-sized teams developing software in the face of vague or rapidly changing requirements." While this statement was true about the origin and intent of XP, it doesn't tell the whole story. In the five years since the publication of the first edition teams have pushed XP much further than the original definition. XP can be described this way:

- ✧ XP is lightweight. In XP you only do what you need to do to create value for the customer. You can't carry a lot of baggage and move fast. However, there is no freeze-dried software process. The body of technical knowledge necessary to be an outstanding team is large and growing.

- ✧ XP is a methodology based on addressing constraints in software development. It does not address project portfolio management, financial justification of projects, operations, marketing, or sales. XP has implications in all of these areas, but does not address these practices directly. Methodology is often interpreted to mean "a set of rules to follow that guarantee success." Methodologies don't work like programs. People aren't computers. Every team does XP differently with varying degrees of success.

- ✧ XP can work with teams of any size. Five years ago, I did not want to claim too much. Others have since put XP to use in a wide range of projects and have had success with both large and small projects and teams. The values and principles behind XP are applicable at any scale. The practices need to be augmented and altered when many people are involved.

- ✧ XP adapts to vague or rapidly changing requirements. XP is still good for this situation, which is fortunate because requirements need to change to adapt to rapid shifts in the modern business world. However, teams have also successfully used XP where requirements don't seem volatile, like porting projects.

XP is my attempt to reconcile humanity and productivity in my own practice of software development and to share that reconciliation. I had begun to notice that the more humanely I treated myself and others, the more productive we all became. The key to success lies not in self-mortification but in acceptance that we are people in a person-to-person business.

Technique also matters. We are technical people in a technical field. There are better ways and worse ways of working. The pursuit of excellence in technique is critical in a social style of development. Technique supports trust relationships. If you can accurately estimate your work, deliver quality the first time, and create rapid feedback loops; then you can be a trustworthy partner. XP demands that participants learn a high level of technique in service of the team's goals.

XP means giving up old habits of working for new ways tailored to today's reality. The habits, attitudes, and values of our early years worked then; but may not be our best choices in the current world of team software development. Good, safe social interaction is as necessary to successful XP development as good technical skills.

One example is the concept that vulnerability is safety. The old habit of holding something back in order to be safe doesn't really work. Holding back that last 20% of effort doesn't protect me. When my project fails, the fact that I didn't give my all doesn't actually make me feel better. It doesn't protect me from a sense of failure that I couldn't make the project work. If I do my very best writing a program and people don't like it, I can still feel justly good about myself. This attitude allows me to feel safe no matter the circumstance. If how I feel is based on an accurate read on whether I did my best, I can feel good about myself by doing my best.

XP teams play full out to win and accept responsibility for the consequences. When self-worth is not tied to the project, we are free to do our best work in any circumstance. In XP you don't prepare for failure. Keeping a little distance in relationships, holding back effort either through underwork or overwork, putting off feedback for another round of responsibility diffusion: none of these behaviors have a place on an XP team.

You may have enough time, money, or skills on your team or you may not; but it is always best to act as if there is going to be enough. This "mentality of sufficiency" is movingly documented by anthropologist Colin Turnbull in *The Mountain People* and *The Forest People*. He contrasts two societies: a resource-starved tribe of lying, cheating backstabbers and a resource-rich, cooperative, loving tribe. I often ask developers in a dilemma, "How would you do it if you had enough time?" You can do your best work even when there are constraints. Fussing about the constraints distracts you from your goals. Your clear self does the best work no matter what the constraints are.

If you have six weeks to get a project done, the only thing you control is your own behavior. Will you get six weeks' worth of work done or less? You can't control others' expectations. You can tell them what you know about the project so their expectations have a chance of matching reality. My terror of deadlines vanished when I learned this lesson. It's not my job to "manage" someone else's expectations. It's their job to manage their own expectations. It's my job to do my best and to communicate clearly.

XP is a software development discipline that addresses risk at all levels of the development process. XP is also productive, produces high-quality software, and is a lot of fun to execute. How does XP address the risks in the development process?

- ✧ Schedule slips—XP calls for short release cycles, a few months at most, so the scope of any slip is limited. Within a release, XP uses one-week iterations of customer-requested features to create fine-grained feedback about progress. Within an iteration, XP plans with short tasks, so the team can solve problems during the cycle. Finally, XP calls for implementing the highest priority features first, so any features that slip past the release will be of lower value.

- ✧ Project canceled—XP asks the business-oriented part of the team to choose the smallest release that makes the most business sense, so there is less to go wrong before deploying and the value of the software is greatest.

- ✧ System goes sour—XP creates and maintains a comprehensive suite of automated tests, which are run and rerun after every change (many times a day) to ensure a quality baseline. XP always keeps the system in deployable condition. Problems are not allowed to accumulate.

- ✧ Defect rate—XP tests from the perspective of both programmers writing tests function-by-function and customers writing tests program-feature-by-program-feature.

- ✧ Business misunderstood—XP calls for business-oriented people to be first-class members of the team. The specification of the project is continuously refined during development, so learning by the customer and the team can be reflected in the software.

⋄ Business changes—XP shortens the release cycle, so there is less change during the development of a single release. During a release, the customer is welcome to substitute new functionality for functionality not yet completed. The team doesn't even notice if it is working on newly discovered functionality or features defined years ago.

⋄ False feature rich—XP insists that only the highest priority tasks are addressed.

⋄ Staff turnover—XP asks programmers to accept responsibility for estimating and completing their own work, gives them feedback about the actual time taken so their estimates can improve, and respects those estimates. The rules for who can make and change estimates are clear. Thus, there is less chance for a programmer to get frustrated by being asked to do the obviously impossible. XP also encourages human contact among the team, reducing the loneliness that is often at the heart of job dissatisfaction. Finally, XP incorporates an explicit model of staff turnover. New team members are encouraged to gradually accept more and more responsibility, and are assisted along the way by each other and by existing programmers.

XP assumes that you see yourself as part of a team, ideally one with clear goals and a plan of execution. XP assumes that you want to work together. XP assumes that change can be made inexpensive using this method. XP assumes that you want to grow, to improve your skills, and to improve your relationships. XP assumes you are willing to make changes to meet those goals.

Now I'm ready to answer the question posed by this chapter: what is XP?

⋄ XP is giving up old, ineffective technical and social habits in favor of new ones that work.

⋄ XP is fully appreciating yourself for total effort today.

⋄ XP is striving to do better tomorrow.

- ✧ XP is evaluating yourself by your contribution to the team's shared goals.
- ✧ XP is asking to get some of your human needs met through software development.

The rest of this book explores what to do to effect these changes and speculates about why they work, personally and economically. The book is divided into two sections. The first is practical, describing a way of doing and thinking about software development that both assumes and satisfies human needs, including the need for relationships. The second section covers the philosophical and historical roots of XP and places XP in today's context.

There are as many ways of reading this book and applying XP as there are of getting into a cool pool on a hot day: one toe at a time, walking steadily down the steps, the cannonball, the racing dive. They all meet the goal of getting into the water. Your choice may be based on style, speed, efficiency, or fear. Only you can decide which is right for you. I hope that in reading and applying this book you will come to a deeper understanding of why you are involved in software development and how you can find satisfaction from this work.

Section 1

Exploring XP

Chapter 2

Learning to Drive

I can remember clearly the day I first began learning to drive. My mother and I were driving up Interstate 5 near Chico, California; a straight, flat stretch of road where the highway stretches right to the horizon. My mom had me reach over from the passenger seat and hold the steering wheel. She let me get the feel of how the motion of the wheel affected the direction of the car. Then she told me, "Here's how you drive. Line the car up in the middle of the lane, straight toward the horizon."

I very carefully squinted straight down the road. I got the car smack dab in the middle of the lane, pointed right down the middle of the road. I was doing great. My mind wandered a little…

I jerked back to attention as the car hit the gravel. My mom (her courage now amazes me) gently got the car back straight on the road. My heart was pounding. Then she actually taught me about driving. "Driving is not about getting the car going in the right direction. Driving is about constantly paying attention, making a little correction this way, a little correction that way."

This is the paradigm for XP. Stay aware. Adapt. Change.

Everything in software changes. The requirements change. The design changes. The business changes. The technology changes. The team changes. The team members change. The problem isn't change, because change is going to happen; the problem, rather, is our inability to cope with change.

There are two levels at which the driving metaphor applies to XP. Customers drive the content of the system. The whole team drives the development process. XP lets you adapt by making frequent, small corrections; moving towards your goal with deployed software at short intervals. You don't wait a long time to find out if you were going the wrong way.

The customers drive the content of the system. Customers (internal or external) start with a general idea of what problems the system needs to solve. However, customers don't usually know exactly what the software should do. That's why software development is like driving, not like getting the car pointed straight down the road. The customers on the team need to keep in mind where on the horizon they want to go even as they decide, week-by-week, where the software should go *next*.

What each team does to express their values will be different from place to place and time to time and team to team. Just as the customers steer the content of the system, the whole team steers the development process, beginning with its current set of practices. As development continues, the team becomes aware of which of their practices enhance and which of their practices detract from their goals. Each practice is an experiment in improving effectiveness, communication, confidence, and productivity.

Chapter 3

Values, Principles, and Practices

What does it take to clearly communicate a new way of thinking about and doing software development? You can learn the basic techniques of gardening quickly from a book, but that doesn't make you a gardener. My friend Paul is a master gardener. I dig and plant and water and weed, but I am not a master gardener.

What are the differences between us? First, Paul knows more techniques than I do, and he's better at the techniques we both know. Technique matters because if you don't dig and plant things, you certainly aren't gardening. Call this level of knowledge and understanding *practices*, things you actually do. Practices are the things you do day-to-day. Specifying practices is useful because they are clear and objective. You either write a test before you change code or you don't. The practices are also useful because they give you a place to start. You can start writing tests before changing code, and gain benefit from doing so, long before you understand software development in a deeper way.

Even if I knew all the same gardening practices as Paul, I still wouldn't be a gardener. Paul has a highly developed sense of what is good and bad about gardening. He can look at a whole garden and get a gut sense of what's working and what isn't. Where I might be proud of my ability to correctly prune a branch, Paul might see that the whole tree should come out. He sees this not because he is a better pruner than I am, but because he has an overall sense of the forces at work in the garden. I have to work at what is simple and obvious to him.

Call this level of knowledge and understanding *values*. Values are the roots of the things we like and don't like in a situation. When a programmer says, "I don't want to estimate my tasks," he generally isn't talking about technique. He already estimates, but doesn't want to reveal what he really thinks for fear of providing a fixed point of judgement that will be used against him later. Better triple that estimate! Refusing to communicate estimates reveals something much deeper about how he sees the social forces in development. Perhaps he doesn't want to be accountable because he has been blamed unfairly in the past. In this case, the programmer values protection over communication. Values are the large-scale criteria we use to judge what we see, think, and do.

Making values explicit is important because without values, practices quickly become rote, activities performed for their own sake but lacking any purpose or direction. When I hear a programmer brush off a defect, I hear a failure of values, not technique. The defect itself might be a failure of technique, but the reluctance to learn from the defect shows that the programmer doesn't actually value learning and self-improvement as much as something else. This is not in the best interest of the program, the organization, or the programmer. Bringing values together with practices means that the programmer can perform a practice, in this case root-cause analysis, at effective times and for good reasons. Values bring purpose to practices.

Practices are evidence of values. Values are expressed at such a high level that I could do just about anything in the name of a value. "I wrote this one-thousand-page document because *I value communication*." Maybe yes and maybe no. If a fifteen minute conversation once a day would have communicated more effectively than producing the document, then the document doesn't show that I value communication. Communicating in the most effective way I can shows I value communication.

Practices are clear. Everyone knows if I've attended the morning standup meetings. Whether I really value communication is fuzzy. Whether I maintain practices that enhance communication is concrete. Just as values bring purpose to practices, practices bring accountability to values.

Values and practices are an ocean apart. Values are universal. Ideally, my values as I work are exactly the same as my values in the rest of my life. Practices, however, are intensely situated. If I want feedback about whether I'm doing a good job programming, continuously building and testing my software makes sense. If I want feedback when I'm changing a diaper, "continuously building and testing" is absurd. The forces involved in the two activities are just too different. To get feedback about my diapering job, I have to pick the baby up when I'm done to see if the diaper falls off. I can't test halfway through. The value "feedback" is expressed in very different forms in the two activities of diapering and programming.

Bridging the gap between values and practices are *principles* (see Figure 1). Principles are domain-specific guidelines for life. Paul's knowledge as a gardener exceeds mine at the level of principles as well. I might know to plant marigolds next to strawberries, but Paul understands the principle of companion planting where adjacent plants make up for each others' weaknesses. Marigolds naturally repel some of the bugs that eat strawberries. Planting them together is a practice. Companion planting is the principle. In this book I present the values, principles, and practices of XP.

This is the limit of what I can communicate in a book. It is a start but it isn't enough for you to master XP. No book of gardening, however complete, makes you a gardener. First you have to garden, then join the community of gardeners, then teach others to garden. Then you are a gardener.

So it is with XP. Reading this book won't make you an extreme programmer. That only comes with programming in the extreme

FIGURE 1.

style, participating in the community of people who share these values and at least some of your practices, and then sharing what you know with others.

You will benefit from studying and trying parts of XP. Learning to write tests before code is useful regardless of your values or the rest of your practices. However, there is as much difference between that and programming extreme as there is between my work in the garden and master gardening.

Chapter 4

Values

Paul, the master gardener, has an intuitive sense of what needs to be done next. He knows in his bones what matters and what doesn't. I might think perfectly straight rows are really important. I put a lot of effort into making my rows straight. Along comes Paul and says, "Why are you working so hard at making the rows straight? What you need is more compost." The difference between what I think is valuable and what is really valuable creates waste.

Everyone who touches software development has a sense of what matters. One person might think what really matters is carefully thinking through all conceivable design decisions before implementing. Another might think what really matters is not having any restrictions on his own personal freedom.

As Will Rogers said, "It ain't what you don't know that gets you in trouble. It's what you know that ain't so." The biggest problem I encounter in what people "just know" about software development is that they are focused on individual action. What actually matters is not how any given person behaves as much as how the individuals behave as part of a team and as part of an organization.

For example, people get passionate about coding style. While there are undoubtedly better styles and worse styles, the most important style issue is that the team chooses to work towards a common style. Idiosyncratic coding styles and the values revealed by them, individual freedom at all costs, don't help the team succeed.

If everyone on the team chooses to focus on what's important to the team, what is it they should focus on? XP embraces five values to guide development: communication, simplicity, feedback, courage, and respect.

Communication

What matters most in team software development is communication. When problems arise in development, most often someone already knows the solution; but that knowledge doesn't get through to someone with the power to make the change. This occurs internally when I ignore my intuition, but the effects are compounded when communicating between people.

Sometimes problems are caused by a lack of knowledge rather than a lack of communication. There's nothing you can do about these problems beforehand, since you didn't know. "Ctrl-shift-S is already assigned in Polish Windows. Who would have thought?" Once you find a surprising problem, communication can help you solve it. You can listen to people who have had similar problems in the past. You can talk as a team about how to make sure the problem doesn't recur.

Perhaps this sounds like a perpetual coffee klatch with everyone sitting around "caring and sharing" and no one doing anything. Other values held by the team keep this from happening. However, motion without communication is not progress.

When you encounter a problem, ask yourselves if the problem was caused by a lack of communication. What communication do you need now to address the problem? What communication do you need to keep yourself out of this trouble in the future?

Communication is important for creating a sense of team and effective cooperation. Communication, though, is not all you need for effective software development.

Simplicity

Simplicity is the most intensely intellectual of the XP values. To make a system simple enough to gracefully solve only today's problem is hard work. Yesterday's simple solution may be fine today, or it may look simplistic or complex. When you need to change to regain simplicity, you must find a way from where you are to where you want to be.

I ask people to think about the question, "What is the simplest thing that could possibly work?" Critics seem to miss the second half of the question. "Well, we have serious security and reliability constraints so we couldn't possibly make our system simple." I'm not asking you to think about what is too simple to work, just to bias your thinking toward eliminating wasted complexity. If security concerns dictate that you split your system across two processors where otherwise you could have used one, as far as I am concerned, that result is simple. The only better solution is if you could find a way to address the security concerns on a single processor.

Simplicity only makes sense in context. If I'm writing a parser with a team that understands parser generators, then using a parser generator is simple. If the team doesn't know anything about parsing and the language is simple, a recursive descent parser is simpler.

The values are intended to balance and support each other. Improving communication helps achieve simplicity by eliminating unneeded or deferrable requirements from today's concerns. Achieving simplicity gives you that much less to communicate about.

Feedback

No fixed direction remains valid for long; whether we are talking about the details of software development, the requirements of the system, or the architecture of the system. Directions set in advance of experience have an especially short half-life. Change is inevitable, but change creates the need for feedback.

I remember an all-day presentation I gave in Aarhus, Denmark. One front-row attendee's face got cloudier and cloudier as the day progressed. Finally he couldn't stand it. "Wouldn't it be easier just to do it right in the first place?" Of course it would, except for three things:

- ✧ We may not know how to do it "right". If we are solving a novel problem there may be several solutions that might work or there may be no clear solution at all.
- ✧ What's right for today may be wrong for tomorrow. Changes outside our control or ability to predict can easily invalidate yesterday's decisions.
- ✧ Doing everything "right" today might take so long that changing circumstances tomorrow invalidate today's solution before it is even finished.

Being satisfied with improvement rather than expecting instant perfection, we use feedback to get closer and closer to our goals. Feedback comes in many forms:

- Opinions about an idea, yours or your teammates'
- How the code looks when you implement the idea
- Whether the tests were easy to write
- Whether the tests run
- How the idea works once it has been deployed

XP teams strive to generate as much feedback as they can handle as quickly as possible. They try to shorten the feedback cycle to minutes or hours instead of weeks or months. The sooner you know, the sooner you can adapt.

It is possible to get too much feedback. If the team is ignoring important feedback; it needs to slow down, frustrating as that may be, until it can respond to the feedback. Then the team can address the underlying issues that caused the excess of feedback. For example, suppose you move to quarterly releases and suddenly have more defect reports than you can respond to before the next quarter's release. Slow down releases until you can handle the defect reports and still develop new functionality. Take the time to figure out why you are creating so many defects or why each defect takes so long to address. Once you've solved the basic problem; you can start releasing quarterly again, cranking up the feedback machine.

Feedback is a critical part of communication. "Is performance going to be a problem?" "I don't know. Let's write a little performance prototype and see." Feedback also contributes to simplicity. Which of three solutions will turn out to be simplest? Try all three and see. While implementing the same thing three times may seem wasteful, it may be the most efficient way to arrive at a solution whose simplicity you can live with. At the same time, the simpler the system, the easier it is to get feedback about it.

Courage

Courage is effective action in the face of fear. Some people have objected to using the word "courage", reserving it for what a patrolling soldier does when going through a darkened doorway. Without intending to diminish the kind of physical courage demonstrated by the soldier, it is certainly true that people involved in software development feel fear. It's how they handle their fear that dictates whether they are working as an effective part of a team.

Sometimes courage manifests as a bias to action. If you know what the problem is, do something about it. Sometimes courage manifests as patience. If you know there is a problem but you don't know what it is, it takes courage to wait for the real problem to emerge distinctly.

Courage as a primary value without counterbalancing values is dangerous. Doing something without regard for the consequences is not effective teamwork. Encourage teamwork by looking to the other values for guidance on what to do when afraid.

If courage alone is dangerous, in concert with the other values it is powerful. The courage to speak truths, pleasant or unpleasant, fosters communication and trust. The courage to discard failing solutions and seek new ones encourages simplicity. The courage to seek real, concrete answers creates feedback.

Respect

The previous four values point to one that lies below the surface of the other four: respect. If members of a team don't care about each other and what they are doing, XP won't work. If members of a team don't care about a project, nothing can save it.

Every person whose life is touched by software development has equal value as a human being. No one is intrinsically worth more than anyone else. For software development to simultaneously improve in humanity and productivity, the contributions of each person on the team need to be respected. I am important and so are you.

Others

Communication, simplicity, feedback, courage, and respect aren't the only possible values for effective software development. Those are the driving values of XP. Your organization, your team, and you yourself may choose other values. What is most important is aligning team behavior to team values. If you do that you can minimize the waste that comes from trying to maintain multiple sets of values simultaneously.

Other important values include safety, security, predictability, and quality-of-life. Holding these values as a team would shape your practices in different ways than the XP values do.

Values don't provide concrete advice about what to *do* in software development. Because of the distance between values and practices, we need a way to bridge the gap between them. Principles are the tool we need. Before jumping into the practices; in the next chapter I introduce the principles of XP, a set of domain-specific guidelines for finding practices in harmony with XP's values.

Chapter 5

Principles

Values are too abstract to directly guide behavior. Long documents are intended to communicate, so are daily conversations. Which is the most effective? The answer depends partly on context and partly on intellectual principles. In this case, the principle of humanity suggests conversation meets the basic human need for connection and so is the preferred form of communication, all other things being equal. Written communication is inherently more wasteful. While written communication allows you to reach a large audience, it is a one-way communication. Conversation allows for clarification, immediate feedback, brainstorming together, and other things you can't do with a document. Written communication tends to be taken as fact or rejected outright, neither of which is an invitation to increased communication.

The principles listed here are not the only possible principles to guide software development. In the development of safety-critical systems, for example, the principle of traceability is at work. At any time you should be able to trace a path from the work done back to an explicitly expressed need from the users. No work should be done for its own sake. If you work in safety-critical systems, the principle of traceability is important for gaining certification for your systems. Because it is not applicable to all software, I did not include it in this list. Other principles may guide your team's practices, but these are the principles that guide XP.

Humanity

People develop software. This simple, inescapable fact invalidates most of the available methodological advice. Often, software development doesn't meet human needs, acknowledge human frailty, and leverage human strength. Acting like software isn't written by people exacts a high cost on participants, their humanity ground away by an inhumane process that doesn't acknowledge their needs. This isn't good for business either, with the costs and disruption of high turnover and missed opportunities for creative action.

What do people need to be good developers?

- Basic safety—freedom from hunger, physical harm, and threats to loved ones. Fear of job loss threatens this need.
- Accomplishment—the opportunity and ability to contribute to their society.
- Belonging—the ability to identify with a group from which they receive validation and accountability and contribute to its shared goals.
- Growth—the opportunity to expand their skills and perspective.
- Intimacy—the ability to understand and be understood deeply by others.

I chose practices for XP because they meet both business and personal needs. There are other human needs; such as rest, exercise, and socialization; that don't need to be met in the work environment. Time away from the team gives each individual more energy and perspective to bring back to the team. Limiting work hours allows time for these other human needs and enhances each person's contribution while he is with the team.

Part of the challenge of team software development is balancing the needs of the individual with the needs of the team. The team's needs may meet your own long-term individual goals, so are worth some amount of sacrifice. Always sacrificing your own needs for the team's doesn't work. If I need privacy, I am responsible for finding a way to get my need met in a way that doesn't hurt the team. The magic of great teams is that after the team members develop trust they find that they are free to be *more* themselves as a result of their work together.

While intimacy feels great, work is still work. Private details of life confuse team communication. I talked to one team in which a member, once he got comfortable on the team, talked about private details of his life every morning. No one else was comfortable hearing about his private life but they didn't know how to confront him. Eventually, the senior team member took him aside and asked him to keep private matters private.

I try to separate my life into private matters that I only discuss with my spouse, personal matters that I discuss with those who have earned my trust, and public matters that I don't mind talking about with anyone. Figuring out which is which is not a simple matter, nor is it simple to figure out who to trust. The rewards of this separation when it works well are effective communication on the job and relationships that are valuable in all aspects of my life.

Economics

Somebody has to pay for all this. Software development that doesn't acknowledge economics risks the hollow victory of a "technical success". Make sure what you are doing has business value, meets business goals, and serves business needs. For example, solving the highest priority business need first maximizes the value of the project.

Two aspects of economics that affect software development are the time value of money and the option value of systems and teams. The time value of money says that a dollar today is worth more than a dollar tomorrow. Software development is more valuable when it earns money sooner and spends money later. Incremental design explicitly defers design investment until the last responsible moment in an effort to spend money later. Pay-per-use provides a way of realizing revenue from features as soon as they are deployed.

Another source of economic value in software development is its value as options for the future. If I can redeploy my media scheduling program for a variety of scheduling-related tasks, it is much more valuable than if it can only be used for its originally intended purpose. All the practices are intended to enhance the option value of both the software and the team while keeping in mind the time value of money by not investing in speculative flexibility.

Mutual Benefit

Every activity should benefit all concerned. Mutual benefit is the most important XP principle and the most difficult to adhere to. There are always solutions to any problem that cost one person while benefitting another. When the situation is desperate, these solutions seem attractive. They are always a net loss, however, because the ill will they create tears down relationships that we need to value. The computer business is really a people business and maintaining working relationships is important.

Extensive internal documentation of software is an example of a practice that violates mutual benefit. I am supposed to slow down my development considerably so some unknown person in a potential future will have an easier time maintaining this code. I can see a possible benefit to the future person should the documentation still happen to be valid, but no benefit now.

XP solves the communication-with-the-future problem in mutually beneficial ways:

- ✧ I write automated tests that help me design and implement better today. I leave these tests for future programmers to use as well. This practice benefits me now and maintainers down the road.
- ✧ I carefully refactor to remove accidental complexity, giving me both satisfaction and fewer defects and making the code easier to understand for those who encounter it later.
- ✧ I choose names from a coherent and explicit set of metaphors which speeds my development and makes the code clearer to new programmers.

If you want people to take your advice, you need to solve more problems than you create. Mutual benefit in XP is searching for practices that benefit me now, me later, and my customer as well. Win-win-win practices are easier to sell because they relieve some immediate pain. For example, someone wrestling with a tough defect is ready to learn test-first programming. When it benefits me now, it is easier to accept doing something to help others both now and in the future.

Self-Similarity

One day I went walking along the Sardinian coast. I saw a little tide pool, maybe two feet across, with the shape outlined in Figure 2. I looked up and noticed that the bay I was walking around, maybe a mile across, had roughly the same shape. "What a great example of the fractal nature of geology," I thought to myself. This drawing is actually a tracing of a map of the whole northwest corner of Sardinia. When nature finds a shape that works, she uses it everywhere she can.

The same principle applies to software development: try copying the structure of one solution into a new context, even at different scales. For example, the basic rhythm of development is that you write a test that fails and then you make it work. The rhythm operates at all different scales. In a quarter, you list the themes you want to address and then you address them with stories. In a week, you list the stories you want to address, write tests expressing the stories, then make them work. In a few hours, you list the tests you know you need to write, then write a test, make it work, write another test, and make them both work until the list is done.

Self-similarity isn't the only principle at work in software development. Just because you copy a structure that works in one context doesn't mean it will work in another. It is a good place to start, though. Likewise, just because a solution is unique doesn't mean it's bad. The situation may really call for a unique solution.

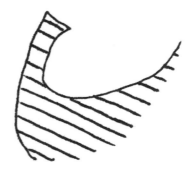

FIGURE 2. **Naturally occurring shape**

In the first edition of *Extreme Programming Explained,* my advice for the weekly cycle was much more like a waterfall: write some code, then test it to make sure it works. I should have paid attention to self-similarity. Having the system-level tests before you begin implementation simplifies design, reduces stress, and improves feedback.

Improvement

In software development, "perfect" is a verb, not an adjective. There is no perfect process. There is no perfect design. There are no perfect stories. You can, however, perfect your process, your design, and your stories.

"Best is the enemy of good enough" suggests that mediocrity is preferable to waiting. This phrase misses the point of XP, which is excellence in software development through improvement. The cycle is to do the best you can today, striving for the awareness and understanding necessary to do better tomorrow. It doesn't mean waiting for perfection in order to begin.

In translating values to practices, the principle of improvement shows in practices that get an activity started right away but refine the results over time. The quarterly cycle is an expression of the possibility of improving long-term plans in the light of experience. Incremental design puts improvement to work by refining the design of the system. The actual design will never be a perfect reflection of the ideal, but you can strive daily to bring the two closer.

The history of software development technology shows us gradually eliminating wasted effort. For example, symbolic assemblers eliminated the wasteful tedium of translating machine instructions into physical bit encodings; "automatic programming" then eliminated the wasteful tedium of translating an abstract description of a program into assembly language; and so on up through automatic storage deallocation.

While our improved technology has eliminated waste, our increased rigidity and specialized social structures in development organizations are increasingly wasteful. The key to improvement is reconciling the two, using newfound technological efficiency to enable new, more effective social relationships. Put improvement to work by not waiting for perfection. Find a starting place, get started, and improve from there.

Diversity

Software development teams where everyone is alike, while comfortable, are not effective. Teams need to bring together a variety of skills, attitudes, and perspectives to see problems and pitfalls, to think of multiple ways to solve problems, and to implement the solutions. Teams need diversity.

Conflict is the inevitable companion of diversity. Not conflict in the "we hate each other and we just can't make progress" sense, but in the "there are two ways to solve this" sense. How do you choose?

Two ideas about a design present an opportunity, not a problem. The principle of diversity suggests that the programmers should work together on the problem and both opinions should be valued.

What if the team isn't good at conflict? Every team has conflict. The question is whether they resolve it productively. Respecting others and maintaining myself smooths communication in times of stress.

Diversity is expressed in the practice of Whole Team, where you bring together on the team people with a variety of skills and perspectives. The various planning cycles encourage people with different perspectives to interact with the goal of creating the most valuable software possible in the time available.

Reflection

Good teams don't just do their work, they think about *how* they are working and *why* they are working. They analyze why they succeeded or failed. They don't try to hide their mistakes, but expose them and learn from them. No one stumbles into excellence.

The quarterly and weekly cycles include time for team reflection, as do pair programming and continuous integration. But reflection should not be limited to "official" opportunities. Conversation with a spouse or friend, vacation, and non-software-related reading and activities all provide individual opportunities to think about how and why you are working the way you are. Shared meals and coffee breaks provide an informal setting for shared reflection.

Reflection isn't a purely intellectual exercise. You can gain insight by analyzing data, but you can also learn from your gut. The "negative" emotions like fear, anger, and anxiety have long provided cues that something bad was about to happen. It takes effort to listen to what your emotions tell you about your work, but feelings tempered by the intellect are a source of insight.

Reflection can be taken too far. Software development has a long tradition of people so busy thinking *about* software development they don't have time to develop software. Reflection comes after action. Learning is action reflected. To maximize feedback, reflection in XP teams is mixed with doing.

Flow

Flow in software development is delivering a steady flow of valuable software by engaging in all the activities of development simultaneously. The practices of XP are biased towards a continuous flow of activities rather than discrete phases.

Software development has long delivered value in big chunks. "Big Bang" integration reflects this tendency. Many teams make the problem worse by tending to respond to stress by making the chunks of value bigger, from deploying software less frequently to integrating less often. Less feedback makes the problem worse, leading to a tendency for even bigger chunks. The more things are deferred, the larger the chunk, the higher the risk. In contrast, the principle of flow suggests that for improvement, deploy smaller increments of value ever more frequently.

A few trends in software development buck the concept of bigger batches. The daily build, for example, is flow-oriented. However, daily builds are a small step on the road to flow. It is not enough that the software compile and link every day; it should also function correctly every day or, better yet, several times a day.

I visited a team that used to deploy every week. It had more and more problems, until it was taking six days to deploy a week's worth of software. The team chose to deploy every two weeks. This amplified their integration and deployment problems. Any time you move away from flow, resolve to return. Resolve the problems that disrupted your flow and get back to weekly deployment as soon as you can.

Opportunity

Learn to see problems as opportunities for change. This isn't to say there are no problems in software development. However, the attitude of "survival" leads to just enough problem solving to get by. To reach excellence, problems need to turn into opportunities for learning and improvement, not just survival.

You might not know what to do about a problem. You might want more time to think about what to do. Sometimes the desire for more time is a mask worn to protect from the fear of the consequences of getting going. Sometimes, though, patience solves a problem by itself.

Turning problems into opportunities takes place across the development process. It maximizes strengths and minimizes weaknesses. Can't make accurate long-term plans? Fine—have a quarterly cycle during which you refine your long-term plans. A person alone makes too many mistakes? Fine—program in pairs. The practices are effective precisely because they address the enduring problems of people developing software together.

As you begin practicing XP, you will certainly encounter problems. Part of being extreme is consciously choosing to transform each problem into an opportunity: an opportunity for personal growth, deepening relationships, and improved software.

Redundancy

Yes, redundancy. The critical, difficult problems in software development should be solved several different ways. Even if one solution fails utterly, the other solutions will prevent disaster. The cost of the redundancy is more than paid for by the savings from not having the disaster.

For example, defects corrode trust and trust is the great waste eliminator. Defects are a critical, difficult problem. Defects are addressed in XP by many of the practices: pair programming, continuous integration, sitting together, real customer involvement, and daily deployment, for example. Even if your partner doesn't catch an error, someone else sitting across the room might or it might be caught by the next integration. Some of these practices are certainly redundant, catching some of the same defects.

You can't solve the defect problem with a single practice. It is too complex, with too many facets, and it will never be solved completely. What you hope to achieve is few enough defects to maintain trust both within the team and with the customer.

While redundancy can be wasteful, be careful not to remove redundancy that serves a valid purpose. Having a testing phase after development is complete should be redundant. However, eliminate it only when it is proven redundant in practice by not finding any defects several deployments in a row.

Failure

If you're having trouble succeeding, fail. Don't know which of three ways to implement a story? Try it all three ways. Even if they all fail, you'll certainly learn something valuable.

Isn't failure waste? No, not if it imparts knowledge. Knowledge is valuable and sometimes hard to come by. Failure may not be avoidable waste. If you knew the best way to implement the story you'd just implement it that way. Given that you don't already know the best way, what's the cheapest way to find out?

I coached a team that had several good designers, so good that each of them could come up with two or three ways of solving any given problem. They would sit for hours, talking about each of their ideas in turn. By the time they were tired of talking, they could have implemented all the alternatives twice. They didn't want to waste programming time, though, so they wasted talking time instead.

I bought the team a kitchen timer and asked them to limit design discussions to fifteen minutes. When the timer went off, two of them would go implement something. They only used the timer a couple of times, but they kept it around as a reminder to fail instead of talk.

This is not intended to excuse failure when you really knew better. When you don't know what to do though, risking failure can be the shortest, surest road to success.

Quality

Sacrificing quality is not effective as a means of control. Quality is not a control variable. Projects don't go faster by accepting lower quality. They don't go slower by demanding higher quality. Pushing quality higher often results in faster delivery; while lowering quality standards often results in later, less predictable delivery.

One of my biggest surprises since the first edition of *Extreme Programming Explained* was released has been just how far teams have been able to push quality as measured in defects, design quality, and the experience of development. Each increase in quality leads to improvements in other desirable project properties, like productivity and effectiveness, as well. There is no apparent limit to the benefits of quality, only limits in our ability to understand how to achieve higher quality.

Quality isn't a purely economic factor. People need to do work they are proud of. I remember talking to the manager of a mediocre team. He went home on the weekends and made fancy ironwork as a blacksmith. He met his need for quality; he just met it outside of work.

If you can't control projects by controlling quality, how can you control them? Time and cost are most often fixed. XP chooses scope as the primary means of planning, tracking, and steering projects. Since scope is never known precisely in advance, it makes a good lever. The weekly and quarterly cycles provide explicit points for tracking and choosing scope.

A concern for quality is no excuse for inaction. If you don't know a clean way to do a job that has to be done, do it the best way you can. If you know a clean way but it would take too long, do the job as well as you have time for now. Resolve to finish doing it the clean way later. This often occurs during architectural evolution, where you have to live with two architectures solving the same problem while you transition from one to the other. Then the transition itself becomes a demonstration of quality: making a big change efficiently in small, safe steps.

Baby Steps

It's always tempting to make big changes in big steps. After all, there's a long way to go and a short time to get there. Momentous change taken all at once is dangerous. It is people who are being asked to change. Change is unsettling. People only change so fast.

I often ask, "What's the least you could do that is recognizably in the right direction?" Baby steps do not justify stasis or glacial change. Under the right conditions, people and teams can take many small steps so rapidly that they appear to be leaping.

Baby steps acknowledge that the overhead of small steps is much less than when a team wastefully recoils from aborted big changes. Baby steps are expressed in practices like test-first programming, which proceeds one test at a time, and continuous integration, which integrates and tests a few hours' worth of changes at a time.

Accepted Responsibility

Responsibility cannot be assigned; it can only be accepted. If someone tries to give you responsibility, only you can decide if you are responsible or if you aren't.

The practices reflect accepted responsibility by, for example, suggesting that whoever signs up to do work also estimates it. Similarly, the person responsible for implementing a story is ultimately responsible for the design, implementation, and testing of the story.

With responsibility comes authority. Misalignments distort the team's communication. When a process expert can tell me how to work, but doesn't share in that work or its consequences, authority and responsibility are misaligned. Neither of us is in an intellectual position to see or use the feedback we need to improve. There is also an emotional cost of living with misalignment.

Conclusion

You can use the principles to understand the practices better and to improvise complementary practices when you don't find one that suits your purpose. While the statement of the practices is intended to be clear and objective (for example "write a test before changing code"), understanding how to apply the practice in your context may not be obvious. The principles give you a better idea of what the practice is intended to accomplish. Also, no fixed list of situated, context-dependent practices covers all of software development. You will create new practices occasionally to fill your specific need. Understanding the principles gives you the opportunity to create practices that work in harmony with your existing practices and your overall goals.

Chapter 6

Practices

Following are the practices of XP, the kind of things you'll see XP teams doing day-to-day. Practices by themselves are barren. Unless given purpose by values, they become rote. Pair programming, for example, makes no sense as a "thing to do to check off a box". Pairing to please your boss is just frustrating. Pair programming to communicate, get feedback, simplify the system, catch errors, and bolster your courage makes a lot of sense.

Practices are situation dependent. If the situation changes, you choose different practices to meet those conditions. Your values do not have to change in order to adapt to a new situation. Some new principles may be called when you change domains.

The practices are stated as absolutes. My intention is to motivate you to aim for perfection, provide you with clear goals, and give you practical ways to get there. The practices are a vector from where you are to where you can be with XP. In XP, you make progress towards this ideal state of effective development. For example, daily deployment may make no sense if you only deploy once a year. Successfully deploying more frequently is an improvement, building confidence for the next step.

Applying a practice is a choice. I think the practices make programming more effective. This is a collection of practices that work and work even better together. They have been used before. Experiment with XP using these practices as your hypotheses. For example, let's try deploying more frequently and see if that helps.

The XP practices do not represent some kind of pinnacle in the evolution of software development. They are a common way station on the road to improvement. The XP practices tend to work well together. Taken one at a time you will likely see improvement. When they begin to compound you may see dramatic improvement. The interactions between the practices amplify their effect.

I have divided the practices into two chapters: "Primary Practices," Chapter 7, and "Corollary Practices," Chapter 9. The primary practices are useful independent of what else you are doing. They each can give you immediate improvement. You can start safely with any of them. The corollary practices are likely to be difficult without first mastering the primary practices. The amplification effect of using the practices together means there is an advantage to adding practices as quickly as you can.

Figure 3 is a summary of the practices:

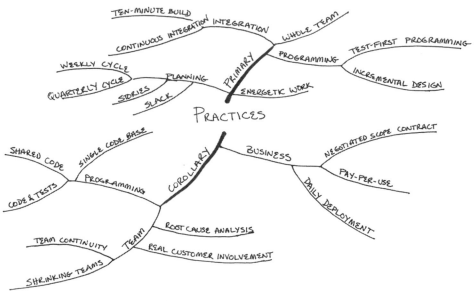

FIGURE 3. Summary of practices

Chapter 7

Primary Practices

In this chapter you'll find practices you can safely start with as you begin to apply XP to improve your software development. Which one you should use first depends completely on your environment and what you perceive as your biggest opportunity for improvement. Some people need planning because they don't know what needs to be done. Some need one of the quality-related practices because they are creating too many defects to be able to see what else is happening.

Sit Together

Develop in an open space big enough for the whole team. Meet the need for privacy and "owned" space by having small private spaces nearby or by limiting work hours so team members can get their privacy needs met elsewhere.

I was called to consult at a floundering project on the outskirts of Chicago. Why the project was floundering was a mystery, because the team consisted of the best technical talent in the company. I walked from cubicle to cubicle trying to figure out what was wrong with their computer program.

After a couple of days, it struck me: I was walking a lot. The senior people of course had corner offices, one in each corner of a floor of a substantial building. The team interacted only a few minutes each day. I suggested that they find a place to sit together. When I returned a month later, the project was humming along. The only space they could find to sit together was in the machine room. They were spending four to five hours a day in a cold, drafty, noisy room; but they were happy because they were successful.

I took two lessons from that experience. One is that no matter what the client says the problem is, it is always a people problem. Technical fixes alone are not enough. The other lesson I took was how important it is to sit together, to communicate with all our senses.

You can creep up on sitting together, if necessary. Put a comfortable chair in your cubicle to encourage conversation. Spend half a day programming in a conference room. Ask for a conference room for a one-week trial of a more open workspace. All of these are steps towards finding a workspace that is effective for your team.

Tearing down the cubicle walls before the team is ready is counterproductive. If the team members' sense of safety is tied to having their own little space, removing that sense of safety before replacing it with the safety of shared accomplishment is likely to produce resentment and resistance. With a little encouragement, teams can shape their own space. A team that knows that physical proximity enhances communication and that has learned the value of communication will open up their own space, given the chance.

Does the practice of sitting together mean that multisite teams can't "do XP"? Chapter 21, "Purity," explores this question in more depth; but the simple answer is no, teams can be distributed and do XP. Practices are theories, predictions. "Sit Together" predicts that the more face time you have, the more humane and productive the project. If you have a multisite project and everything is going well, keep doing what you're doing. If you have problems, think about ways to sit together more, even if it means traveling.

Whole Team

Include on the team people with all the skills and perspectives necessary for the project to succeed. This is really nothing more than the old idea of cross-functional teams. The name reflects the purpose of the practice, a sense of wholeness on the team, the ready availability of all the resources necessary to succeed. Where intense interactions are necessary for the health of the project, those interacting should be primarily identified with the team and not their functions.

People need a sense of "team":

- ✧ We belong.
- ✧ We are in this together.
- ✧ We support each others' work, growth, and learning.

What constitutes a "whole team" is dynamic. If a set of skills or attitudes becomes important, bring a person with these skills on the team. If someone is no longer necessary, he can go elsewhere. For example, if your project requires many changes to a database, you will need a database administrator on the team. When the need for database changes diminishes that person no longer needs to be part of the team, at least for that function.

An issue that often arises is ideal team size. *The Tipping Point* by Malcolm Gladwell describes two discontinuities in team size: 12 and 150. Many organizations; military, religious, and business; split teams when they cross these thresholds. Twelve is the number of people who can comfortably interact with each other in a day. With more than 150 people on a team, you can no longer recognize the faces of everyone on your team. Across both of these thresholds it is harder to maintain trust, and trust is necessary for collaboration. For larger projects, finding ways to fracture the problem so it can be solved by a team of teams allows XP to scale up.

Some organizations try to have teams with fractional people: "You'll spend 40% of your time working for these customers and 60% work for those customers." In this case, so much time is wasted on task-switching that you can see immediate improvement by grouping the programmers into teams. The team responds to the customers' needs. This frees the programmers from fractured thinking. The customer receives the benefit of the expertise of the whole team as needed. People need acceptance and belonging. Identifying with this program on Mondays and Thursdays and that program on Tuesdays, Wednesdays, and Fridays, without having other programmers to identify with, destroys the sense of "team" and is counterproductive.

Informative Workspace

Make your workspace about your work. An interested observer should be able to walk into the team space and get a general idea of how the

FIGURE 4. Stories on a wall

project is going in fifteen seconds. He should be able to get more information about real or potential problems by looking more closely.

Many teams implement this practice in part by putting story cards on a wall. Sorting the cards spatially conveys information quickly. If the "Done" area isn't collecting cards, what does the team needs to improve in its planning, estimation, or execution? I'll also wonder what customers need to be involved so the slipping scope has minimal business impact. Figure 4 shows an idealized story wall with spatially sorted stories.

The workspace (Figure 5) also needs to provide for other human needs. Water and snacks provide comfort and encourage positive social interactions. Cleanliness and order leave minds free to think

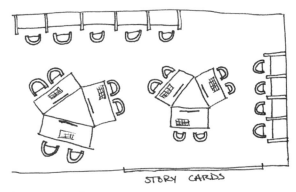

FIGURE 5. A team workspace

about the problems at hand. While programming happens in a public space people also need privacy, which can be provided by separate cubes or by limiting work hours.

Another implementation of the informative workspace is big, visible charts. If you have an issue that requires steady progress, begin charting it. Once the issue is resolved, or if the chart stops getting updated, take it down. Use your space for important, active information.

Energized Work

Work only as many hours as you can be productive and only as many hours as you can sustain. Burning yourself out unproductively today and spoiling the next two days' work isn't good for you or the team.

Where does the penchant for long hours come from? I'm often asked for "scientific" evidence for the practices in XP, as if science could somehow bear the responsibility for project success or failure. Work hours are one area where I wish I could turn this argument around. Where is the scientific evidence that members of a software team produce more value in eighty hour weeks than in forty hour weeks? Software development is a game of insight, and insight comes to the prepared, rested, relaxed mind.

In my own case I think I turn to long work hours as a way of grabbing control in a situation in which I am otherwise out of control. I can't control how the whole project is going; I can't control whether the product sells; but I can always stay later. With enough caffeine and sugar, I can keep typing long past the point where I have started removing value from the project. It's easy to remove value from a software project; but when you're tired, it's hard to recognize that you're removing value.

When you're sick, respect yourself and the rest of your team by resting and getting well. Taking care of yourself is the quickest way back to energized work. You also protect the team from losing more productivity because of illness. Coming in sick doesn't show commitment to work, because when you do you aren't helping the team.

You can make incremental improvements in work hours. Stay at work the same amount of time but manage that time better. Declare a two-hour stretch each day as Code Time. Turn off the phones and email notification, and just program for two hours. That may be enough improvement for now and may set the stage for fewer hours at work later.

Pair Programming

Write all production programs with two people sitting at one machine. Set up the machine so the partners can sit comfortably side-by-side. Move the keyboard and mouse back and forth so you are comfortable while you are typing. Pair programming is a dialog between two people simultaneously programming (and analyzing and designing and testing) and trying to program better. Pair programmers:

 ✧ Keep each other on task.
 ✧ Brainstorm refinements to the system.
 ✧ Clarify ideas.
 ✧ Take initiative when their partner is stuck, thus lowering frustration.
 ✧ Hold each other accountable to the team's practices.

Pairing doesn't mean that you can't think alone. People need both companionship and privacy. If you need to work on an idea alone, go do it. Then come back and check in with your team. You can even prototype alone and still respect pairing. However, this is not an excuse to act outside of the team. When you're done exploring, bring the resulting idea, not the code, back to the team. With a partner, you'll reimplement it quickly. The results will be more widely understood, benefitting the project as a whole.

Pair programming is tiring but satisfying. Most programmers can't pair for more than five or six hours in a day. After a week like that, they are ready for a relaxing weekend away from work. I keep a bottle of water beside me while I pair. It's good for my health and I'm eventually reminded to take a break. The breaks keep me fresh for the whole day.

Rotate pairs frequently. Some teams report good results obeying a timer that tells them to shift partners every sixty minutes (every thirty minutes when solving difficult problems). I don't think I'd like this, but I haven't tried it. I like to program with someone new every couple of hours, switching at natural breaks in development.

Pairing and Personal Space

An issue that has come up and requires comment is the close contact in pair programming. Different individuals and cultures are comfortable with different amounts of body space. Pairing with an Italian who communicates best when very close is completely different than pairing with a Dane who likes a few feet of personal space. If you aren't aware of the difference it can be acutely uncomfortable. Personal space must be respected for both parties to work well.

Personal hygiene and health are important issues when pairing. Cover your mouth when you cough. Don't come to work when you are sick. Avoid strong colognes that might affect your partner.

Working effectively together feels good. It may be a new experience in the workplace for some. When programmers aren't emotionally mature enough to separate approval from arousal, working with a person of the opposite gender can bring up sexual feelings that are not in the best interest of the team. If these feelings arise when pairing, stop pairing with the person until you have taken responsibility for and dealt with your feelings. Even if the feelings are mutual, acting on them will hurt the team. If you want to have an intimate relationship, one of you should leave the team so you can build a personal relationship in a personal setting without confusing the team's communication with a sexual subtext. Ideally, emotions at work will be about work.

It is important to respect individual differences when pairing. In Figure 6 the man has moved closer to the woman than is comfortable for her. Neither is making his or her best technical decisions at this point, although they may be completely unaware of the source of their discomfort.

If you are uncomfortable pairing with someone on the team, talk about it with someone safe; a respected team member, a manager, or someone in human resources. If you aren't comfortable, the team isn't doing as well as it could. And chances are others are uncomfortable too.

FIGURE 6. Personal space and pairing

Stories

Plan using units of customer-visible functionality. "Handle five times the traffic with the same response time." "Provide a two-click way for users to dial frequently used numbers." As soon as a story is written, try to estimate the development effort necessary to implement it.

Software development has been steered wrong by the word "requirement", defined in the dictionary as "something mandatory or obligatory." The word carries a connotation of absolutism and permanence, inhibitors to embracing change. And the word "requirement" is just plain wrong. Out of one thousand pages of "requirements", if you deploy a system with the right 20% or 10% or even 5%, you will likely realize all of the business benefit envisioned for the whole system. So what were the other 80%? Not "requirements"; they weren't really mandatory or obligatory.

Early estimation is a key difference between stories and other requirements practices. Estimation gives the business and technical perspectives a chance to interact, which creates value early, when an idea has the most potential. When the team knows the cost of features it can split, combine, or extend scope based on what it knows about the features' value.

Give stories short names in addition to a short prose or graphical description. Write the stories on index cards and put them on a frequently-passed wall. Figure 7 is a sample card of a story I wish my scanner program implemented. Every attempt I've seen to computerize stories has failed to provide a fraction of the value of having real cards on a real wall. If you need to report progress to other parts of the organization in a familiar format, translate the cards into that format periodically.

One feature of XP-style planning is that stories are estimated very early in their life. This gets everyone thinking about how to get the greatest return from the smallest investment. If someone asks me whether I want the Ferrari or the minivan, I choose the Ferrari. It will inevitably be more fun. However, as soon as someone says, "Do you want the Ferrari for $150,000 or the minivan for $25,000?" I can begin to make an informed decision. Adding new constraints like "I need to haul five children" or "It has to go 150 miles per hour" clear the picture further. There are cases where either decision makes sense. You can't make a good decision based on image alone. To choose a car wisely you need to know your constraints, both cost and intended use. All other things being equal, appeal comes into play.

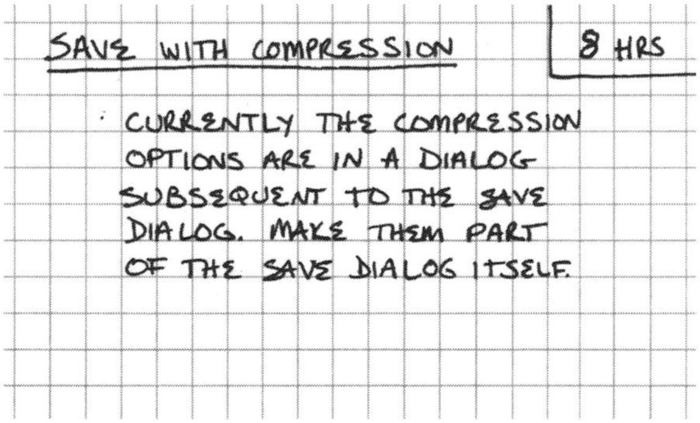

FIGURE 7. Sample story card

Weekly Cycle

Plan work a week at a time. Have a meeting at the beginning of every week. During this meeting:

1. Review progress to date, including how actual progress for the previous week matched expected progress.
2. Have the customers pick a week's worth of stories to implement this week.
3. Break the stories into tasks. Team members sign up for tasks and estimate them.

Start the week by writing automated tests that will run when the stories are completed. Then spend the rest of the week completing the stories and getting the tests to pass. A team proud of its work will fully implement the stories, not just do enough work to get the tests to pass. The goal is to have deployable software at the end of the week which everyone can celebrate as progress.

The week is a widely shared time scale. The nice thing about a week as opposed to two or three (as I recommended in the first edition) is that everyone is focused on Friday. The team's job—programmers, testers, and customers together—is to write the tests and then get them to run in five days. If you get to Wednesday and it is clear that all the tests won't be running, that the stories won't be completed and ready to deploy, you still have time to choose the most valuable stories and complete them.

Some people like to start their week on a Tuesday or Wednesday. I was surprised when I first saw it, but it's common enough to mention. As one manager told me, "Monday's are unpleasant and planning is unpleasant, so why put them together?" I don't think planning should be unpleasant; but in the meantime, shifting the start of the cycle makes some sense as long as it doesn't put pressure on people to work over the weekend. Working weekends is not sustainable; if the real problem is that the estimates are overly optimistic, then work on improving your estimates.

Planning is a form of necessary waste. It doesn't create much value all by itself. Work on gradually reducing the percentage of time you spend planning. Some teams start with a whole day of planning for a week, but gradually refine their planning skills until they spend an hour planning for the week.

I like to break stories into tasks that individuals take responsibility for and estimate. I think ownership of tasks goes a long way towards satisfying the human need for ownership. I've seen other styles work well, though. You can write small stories that eliminate the need for separate tasks. The cost of this approach is more work for the customer. You can also eliminate sign-up by keeping a stack of tasks. When a programmer is ready to start a new task, he takes one from the top of the stack. This eliminates the opportunity for him to choose a task he particulary cares about or is especially good at, but ensures that each programmer gets a variety of tasks. (Pairing gives programmers a chance to use specialist skills, whocvcr holds the task.)

The weekly heartbeat also gives you a convenient, frequent, and predictable platform for team and individual experiments. "OK, for the next week we're going to switch pair partners every hour on the hour," or "I'll juggle for five minutes every morning before I start programming."

Quarterly Cycle

Plan work a quarter at a time. Once a quarter reflect on the team, the project, its progress, and its alignment with larger goals.

During quarterly planning:

✧ Identify bottlenecks, especially those controlled outside the team.
✧ Initiate repairs.
✧ Plan the theme or themes for the quarter.
✧ Pick a quarter's worth of stories to address those themes.
✧ Focus on the big picture, where the project fits within the organization.

A season is another natural, widely shared timescale to use in organizing time for a project. Using a quarter as a planning horizon synchronizes nicely with other business activities that occur quarterly. Quarters are also a comfortable interval for interaction with external suppliers and customers.

The separation of "themes" from "stories" is intended to address the tendency of the team to get focused and excited about the details of what they are doing without reflecting on how this week's stories fit into the bigger picture. Themes also fit well into larger-scale planning such as drawing marketing roadmaps.

Quarters are also a good interval for team reflection, finding gnawing-but-unconscious bottlenecks. You can also propose and evaluate long-running experiments quarterly.

Slack

In any plan, include some minor tasks that can be dropped if you get behind. You can always add more stories later and deliver more than you promised. It is important in an atmosphere of distrust and broken promises to meet your commitments. A few met commitments go a long way toward rebuilding relationships.

In Iceland, one of the winter sports is taking monstrous trucks bouncing around the backcountry. These trucks all have four-wheel-drive; but when they are out crashing around, they only use two-wheel-drive. If they get stuck in two-wheel-drive they have four-wheel-drive to get them out. If they get stuck in four-wheel-drive they're just stuck.

I remember two conversations: one with a middle manager who had one hundred people reporting to him and another with his executive manager who had three hundred people in his organization. I suggested to the middle manager that he encourage his teams to only sign up for what they were confident they could actually do. They had a long history of overcommitting and underdelivering. "Oh, I couldn't do that. If I don't agree to aggressive [i.e. unrealistic] schedules, I'll be fired." The next day, I talked to the executive. "Oh, they never come in on time. It's okay. They still deliver enough of what we need."

I had been watching first-hand the incredible waste generated by their habitual overcommitment: unmanageable defect loads, dismal morale, and antagonistic relationships. Meeting commitments, even modest ones, eliminates waste. Clear, honest communication relieves tension and improves credibility.

You can structure slack in many ways. One week in eight could be "Geek Week". Twenty percent of the weekly budget could go to programmer-chosen tasks. You may have to begin slack with yourself, telling yourself how long you actually think a task will take and giving yourself time to do it, even if the rest of the organization is not ready for honest and clear communication.

Ten-Minute Build

Automatically build the whole system and run all of the tests in ten minutes. A build that takes longer than ten minutes will be used much less often, missing the opportunity for feedback. A shorter build doesn't give you time to drink your coffee.

Physics has reassuringly concrete natural constants. At sea level on earth, the force of gravity accelerates objects at 9.8 meters per second per second. You can count on gravity. Software has few such certainties. The ten-minute build is as close as we get in software engineering. I've observed several teams that started with an automated build-and-test process never letting the process take longer than ten minutes. If it did, someone optimized it but only until it took ten minutes again.

The ten-minute build is an ideal. What do you do on your way to that ideal? The statement of the practice gives three clues: *automatically* build the *whole* system and run *all* of the tests in ten minutes. If your process isn't automated, that's the first place to start. Then you may be able to build only the part of the system you have changed. Finally, you may be able to run only tests covering the part of the system at risk because of the changes you made.

Any guess about what parts of the system *need* to be built and what parts *need* to be tested introduces the risk of error. If you are wrong, you may miss unpredictable errors with all of their social and economic costs. However, being able to test some of the system is much better than being able to test none at all.

Automated builds are much more valuable than builds requiring manual intervention. As the general stress level rises, manual builds tend to be done less often and less well, resulting in more errors and more stress. Practices should lower stress. An automated build becomes a stress reliever at crunch time. "Did we make a mistake? Let's just build and see."

Continuous Integration

Integrate and test changes after no more than a couple of hours. Team programming isn't a divide and conquer problem. It is a divide, conquer, and integrate problem. The integration step is unpredictable, but can easily take more time than the original programming. The longer you wait to integrate, the more it costs and the more unpredictable the cost becomes.

The most common style of continuous integration is asynchronous. I check in my changes. Soon thereafter, the build system notices the change and starts to build and test. If there are problems; I am notified by email, text message, or (most coolly) a glowing red lava lamp.

I prefer a synchronous model in which my partner and I integrate after each pair-programming episode, no more than a couple of hours. We wait for the build to complete and the entire test suite to run with no regressions before proceeding.

Asynchronous integrations are a big improvement on daily builds (especially without automated tests), but they don't have the inherent reflection time built into the synchronous style. Waiting for the compiler and the tests is a natural time to talk about what we've just done together and how we might have done it better. Synchronous builds also create positive pressure for a short, clear feedback cycle. When I get notified of a problem half an hour after starting a new task; I waste a lot of time remembering what I was doing, fixing the problem, and then finding my place in the interrupted task.

Integrate and build a complete product. If the goal is to burn a CD, burn a CD. If the goal is to deploy a web site, deploy a web site, even if it is to a test environment. Continuous integration should be complete enough that the eventual first deployment of the system is no big deal.

Test-First Programming

Write a failing automated test before changing any code. Test-first programming addresses many problems at once:

- Scope creep—It's easy to get carried away programming and put in code "just in case." By stating explicitly and objectively what the program is supposed to do, you give yourself a focus for your coding. If you really want to put that other code in, write another test after you've made this one work.

- Coupling and cohesion—If it's hard to write a test, it's a signal that you have a design problem, not a testing problem. Loosely coupled, highly cohesive code is easy to test.

✧ Trust—It's hard to trust the author of code that doesn't work. By writing clean code that works and demonstrating your intentions with automated tests, you give your teammates a reason to trust you.

✧ Rhythm—It's easy to get lost for hours when you are coding. When programming test-first, it's clearer what to do next: either write another test or make the broken test work. Soon this develops into a natural and efficient rhythm—test, code, refactor, test, code, refactor.

The XP community hasn't done much exploration of alternatives to tests for verifying the behavior of the system. Tools like static analysis and model checking could be used test-first style. You start with a "test" that says, for example, that there are no deadlocks in the system. After every change, you verify again that there are no deadlocks. The static analysis tools I've seen aren't intended to be used this way. They run too slowly to be part of the minute-by-minute cycle of programming. However, this seems to be merely a matter of focus, not a fundamental limitation.

Another refinement of test-first programming is continuous testing, first reported by David Saff and Michael Ernst in "An Experimental Evaluation of Continuous Testing During Development," and also explored in Erich Gamma's and my book *Contributing to Eclipse*. In continuous testing the tests are run on every program change, much as an incremental compiler is run on every change to the source code. Test failures are reported in the same format as compiler errors. Continuous testing reduces the time to fix errors by reducing the time to discover them. The tests have to run quickly, however.

The tests you write while coding test-first have the limitation that they take a microview of the program: do these two objects work well together? As your experience grows, you'll be able to squeeze more and more reassurance into these tests. Because of their limited scope, these tests tend to run very fast. You can run thousands of them as part of the Ten-Minute Build.

Incremental Design

Invest in the design of the system every day. Strive to make the design of the system an excellent fit for the needs of the system that day. When your understanding of the best possible design leaps forward, work gradually but persistently to bring the design back into alignment with your understanding.

I was taught exactly the opposite of this strategy in school: "Put in all the design you can before you begin implementation because you'll never get another chance." The intellectual justification for this strategy came from a Barry Boehm study of 1960's defense contracts showing that the cost of fixing defects rose exponentially over time. If the same data also hold for adding features to today's software, then the cost of large-scale design changes should rise dramatically over time. In that case, the most economical design strategy is to make big design decisions early and defer all small-scale decisions until later.

For an assumption that shaped software development orthodoxy for decades, the increasing cost of change over time received little scrutiny. This assumption may no longer be valid. Do changes also increase in cost, the same way defects do? Even assuming changes do increase in cost sometimes, are there conditions under which the cost of changes does not increase? If changes do not grow increasingly expensive, what does that imply about the best way to develop software?

XP teams work hard to create conditions under which the cost of changing the software doesn't rise catastrophically. The automated tests, the continual practice of improving the design, and the explicit social process all contribute to keep the cost of changes low.

XP teams are confident in their ability to adapt the design to future requirements. Because of this, XP teams can meet their human need for immediate and frequent success as well as their economic need to defer investment to the last responsible moment. Some of the teams who read and applied the first edition of this book didn't get the part of the message about the last *responsible* moment. They piled story on story as quickly as possible with the least possible investment in design. Without daily attention to design, the cost of changes does skyrocket. The result is poorly designed, brittle, hard-to-change systems.

The advice to XP teams is not to minimize design investment over the short run, but to keep the design investment in proportion to the needs of the system so far. The question is not whether or not to design, the question is when to design. Incremental design suggests that the most effective time to design is in the light of experience.

If small, safe steps are *how* to design, the next question is *where* in the system to improve the design. The simple heuristic I have found helpful is to eliminate duplication. If I have the same logic in two places, I work with the design to understand how I can have only one copy. Designs without duplication tend to be easy to change. You don't find yourself in the situation where you have to change the code in several places to add one feature.

As a direction for improvement, incremental design doesn't say that designing in advance of experience is horrible. It says that design done close to when it is used is more efficient. As your expertise grows in making changes to a running system in small, safe steps, you can afford to defer more and more of the design investment. As you do so, the system will get simpler, progress will start sooner, tests will be easier to write, and because the system is smaller there will be less to communicate with the team.

As more teams invest in daily design, they notice that the changes they are making are similar regardless of the purpose of the system. Refactoring is a discipline of design that codifies these recurring patterns of changes. These refactorings can occur at any level of scale. Few design decisions are difficult to change once made. The result is systems that can start small and grow as needed without exorbitant cost.

And Now...

The practices in this chapter aren't the whole story of XP. They provide a foundation of respect, communication, and feedback that fosters simplicity and courage. The team members can use their increasing confidence and competence to build relationships inside and outside the team.

The big payoff of XP comes once these practices are firmly in place. Then comes the big step forward: business relationships that directly support further perfection of software development.

Chapter 8

Getting Started

You are already developing software. You have already started. XP is a way to improve both your development process and your experience of it. To do XP, you start where you are and adapt by adding practices that meet your goals and express your values. As you add practices, the synergies between them make things possible that you previously couldn't imagine. And then, you want more. By the time you have applied XP completely you are energized, confident, part of an active community, and working at a seemingly incredible pace with less stress than ever before.

XP may represent a new direction or an acceleration in your efforts to improve. If so, how and where do you start?

First, there is no one right place for everyone to start. Any of the primary practices are safe, offering immediate improvement if you have the problem they are designed to address. Feeling overwhelmed by everything you have to do? Start the weekly cycle for yourself. Take time at the beginning of the week to write down everything you think you can accomplish in the week. If there is too much to do, align your priorities with the team's needs.

It's easy to start by changing one thing at a time. I think it's hard to jump in and do all the practices, embrace all the values, and apply all the principles in novel circumstances by reading this book and deciding to do it. The technical skills in XP and the attitudes behind them take a while to learn. XP works best when it is done all together, but you need a starting place.

Change is not necessarily slow. A team eager or desperate for improvement can progress quickly. It doesn't need to wait long to assimilate one change before moving on to the next practice. If you change too fast, though, you risk slipping back into old practices and values. When this happens, take time to regroup. Remind yourself of the values you want to hold. Review your practices and remind yourself why you chose them. New habits take time to solidify.

How do you decide what to change first? Look at what you are doing and what you want to achieve. Choose the first practice on that path. One option is to use XP-style planning. Write stories about improving your software development process. "Automate the build." "Test first all day." "Pair program with Joe for two hours." Estimate how long each will take. Figure out your budget for process improvement. Pick a story to work on first. Adapt as you discover what is easy or valuable and what is difficult.

I've used this same process myself with organizations planning to apply XP. One team's stories were about teaching classes, trying pilot projects, and educating executives. Our sponsors asked for instant change even though everyone knew that wasn't possible. Applying XP-style planning to the process of change let us communicate and align our priorities and gave our sponsors a chance to see what we were doing and influence what was happening.

Change begins with awareness. Awareness of the need for change comes from feelings, instincts, facts, or feedback from outsiders. Feelings, while valuable, need to be cross-checked with facts or trusted opinions.

Metrics can lead to awareness. Trends in metrics can point to the need for change before the consequence of the trend becomes painful. I coached a team that went through all of its post-development defects and discovered that they had all been created by individuals programming alone. Without the ability to reflect accurately on its experience, the team wouldn't have been able to make an informed decision about how much to pair program.

Once you are aware of the need for change, you can begin to change. The primary practices are possible places to begin improving your development practices. Each describes a continuum of behavior. Find your current position with respect to each of the practices. Pick a practice whose purpose matches your own priorities for change. Move one step closer to the endpoint illustrating the practice. See if the humanity and effectiveness of your development improves.

For example, I might decide that I need closer technical collaboration. I have a big integration coming up and I am feeling increasingly nervous in spite of design and code reviews. How can I collaborate more?

Pair programming is the practice that addresses technical collaboration. At full intensity, it suggests that all long-lived code be written by two people having a conversation as they program. Perhaps my team is not willing to "give up" that much time, since we are all going to be held personally responsible for our areas of the code. However, I can collaborate one step more intensely by picking a piece of code about which I am nervous and asking someone else to pair with me for an hour or two as I work out its interface to another part of the system. I would be wise to choose the person responsible for the other part of the system as my partner, if he is willing.

Once we've paired, we can evaluate whether closer technical collaboration helped or hindered our team's accomplishment of its goals. We're in an informed position to decide whether to further intensify our collaboration and what means to use: pairing, reviews, or some other method.

Once I change, sometimes I want the familiarity of an old way of working more than the improvement of a new way. Even if I change, the people I relate to may resist my changes enough that I would rather change back than hold myself to my new standards. Complicating the situation is my own insecurity about my new practices. Do I program faster or slower if I write automated tests along with my programs? I want to avoid changing back inappropriately.

Change always starts at home. The only person you can actually change is yourself. No matter how functional or dysfunctional your organization, you can begin applying XP for yourself. Anyone on the team can begin changing his own behavior. Programmers can start writing tests first. Testers can automate their tests. Customers can write stories and set clear priorities. Executives can expect transparency.

Dictating practices to a team destroys trust and creates resentment. Executives can encourage team responsibility and accountability. Whether the team produces these with XP, a better waterfall, or utter chaos is up to them. Using XP, teams can produce dramatic improvements in the areas of defects, estimation, and productivity. The price of the improvement is closer collaboration and engagement with the whole team. Raise your expectations for accountability and teamwork, then help the team through the inevitable anxiety that comes with change.

Mapping the Practices

Here is an exercise for discovering what each practice means for you and your team.

Figure 8 is a map of the Energetic Work practice. In the middle is the practice. Directly below that is the purpose of the practice as I see it: to keep my work and my life in balance. Attached to the practice are factors that affect it and, in this case, symptoms that the practice isn't going well. Map whatever issues come to mind when you think about a practice. Be as textual or graphical as you like.

There are no "right" answers in this exercise. The example contains my answers for today. Each team member and each team will interpret what the practice means differently. The discussion around what is attached to the practice is one valuable side effect of the exercise.

Once you have potential changes to make, make some of them. All the good ideas about how to make things better are useless unless they release energy for change. I've sat through far too many "crying in the beer" sessions where all the energy for change was dissipated in the intensity of the complaining. Once you see an idea for improvement that makes sense to you, do it. If you can do it as a team, so much the

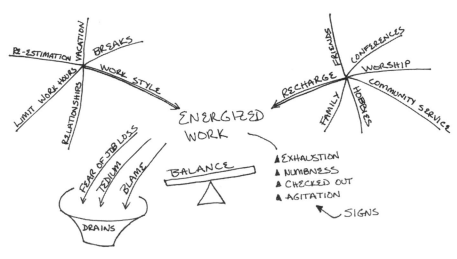

FIGURE 8. Map of Energetic Work

better. If not, do it alone until you can share what you've learned with someone you trust.

I recommend taking up to half a day to go through all of the practices and deciding together what would constitute change with respect to each of them. Put the resulting maps on flip charts and post them around the team room. When one change is in place, look to see what new changes may have come into reach and begin working on them.

Conclusion

If there is one message I would like to communicate, whatever your job title and however your work is touched by software development, it is this: software development is capable of much, much more than it is currently delivering. Defects should be notable because they are rare. Major scope adjustments because of lack of progress should only need to occur in the first half of schedules. Initial deployment of software should come after a small percentage of the project budget is spent. Teams should be able to grow and shrink without catastrophic consequences. XP is a way to get to that place. When we work with human nature in our development process, we have the opportunity to make these big leaps in effectiveness.

Chapter 9

Corollary Practices

The practices in this chapter seem to me to be difficult or dangerous to implement before completing the preliminary work of the primary practices. If you begin deploying daily, for example, without getting the defect rate down close to zero (with pair programming, continuous integration, and test-first programming); you will have a disaster on your hands. Trust your nose about what you need to improve next. If one of the following practices seems appropriate, give it a try. It might work or you might discover that you have more work to do before you can use it to improve your development process.

Real Customer Involvement

Make people whose lives and business are affected by your system part of the team. Visionary customers can be part of quarterly and weekly planning. They can have a budget, a percentage of the available development capacity, to do with as they please. If this is the kind of customer who encounters problems six months before the rest of the market, making the system they want can put you ahead of your competition. If your product is valuable to them, they may be willing to pay for their participation. The point of customer involvement is to reduce wasted effort by putting the people with the needs in direct contact with the people who can fill those needs.

Whole Team seems to me to imply customer involvement, but I haven't seen many teams go as far as they could toward involving real customers. You will get different results with real customers. They are who you are trying to please. No customer at all, or a "proxy" for a real customer, leads to waste as you develop features that aren't used, specify tests that don't reflect the real acceptance criteria, and lose the chance to build real relationships between the people with the most diverse perspectives of the project.

The objection I hear to customer involvement is that someone will get exactly the system he wants, but the system won't be suitable for anyone else. It's easier to generalize a successful system than to specialize a system that doesn't solve anyone's problem. Ensuring that the system stays generally useful is the job of the marketing members of the team. Generally, the closer customer needs and development capabilities are, the more valuable development becomes.

"The sausage factory" is another objection to customer involvement. "If the customers knew how messed up software development was, they'd never trust us." Are you sure they trust you now? Software reflects the organization that builds it. The customers are already using the software so they already know a lot about how you develop. If they don't yet, they will soon. When you act trustworthy and have nothing to hide, you are more productive. (Think of all the time you no longer have to spend hiding or covering up.) When you are ready with accurate estimates and low defect rates, including customers in the development process fosters trust and encourages continued improvement.

Incremental Deployment

When replacing a legacy system, gradually take over its workload beginning very early in the project. I was talking with a friend recently about a grocery chain that was planning to switch from its sophisticated home-grown software to a package. The plan was to reimplement the current functionality in the package and then cut over one Sunday night. My instant response was, "That trick never works."

Every once in a while a big deployment works. You spend months not adding any new functionality just getting ready for D-Day. People work long hours and weekends. If the bet pays off and the new system runs well enough, everyone is too exhausted to return to productive development for weeks or months. And if the bet doesn't pay off and the new system has to be pulled, the costs are even higher. Big deployments have a high risk and high human and economic costs.

What's the alternative? Find a little piece of functionality or a limited data set you can handle right away. Deploy it. You'll have to find a way to run both programs in parallel, splitting and merging files or training some users to use both programs. This scaffolding, technical or social, is the price you pay for insurance.

I used to believe in incremental deployment in my head, not my gut. A job helping to migrate nine thousand contracts to a new system changed my mind. After a couple of months we could handle 80% of the contracts, but because of data quality problems we couldn't match the answers for the other 20%. We spent six months trying to get the rest of the contracts working, including duplicating the errors in the old system. (You wouldn't believe what they did to round floating-point numbers!) Then our manager changed priorities and asked us to convert a different set of contracts. At the end of the year we hadn't gotten any of the contracts deployed in the new system and I lost a bonus equal to the cost of a new house. Now I *really, really* believe in incremental deployment.

Team Continuity

Keep effective teams together. There is a tendency in large organizations to abstract people to things, plug-compatible programming units. Value in software is created not just by what people know and do but also by their relationships and what they accomplish together. Ignoring the value of relationships and trust just to simplify the scheduling problem is false economy.

Small organizations don't have this problem. There is only one team. Once you gel, once you earn and offer trust, nothing short of shared calamity can pull the team apart. Large organizations often ignore the value in teams, adopting instead a molecular/fluid metaphor for "programming resources". Once a project is done they go back "into the pool". The goal of such scheduling is to get all the programmers fully utilized. This strategy maximizes micro-efficiency but undermines the efficiency of the organization as a whole, striving for the illusory efficiency of keeping individuals busy typing while ignoring the value of enabling people to work mostly with those they know and trust.

Keeping gelled teams together doesn't mean that teams are entirely static. I have been astonished at how quickly new members begin contributing to established XP teams. They insist on signing up for tasks the first week and they are independently contributing after a month. By mostly keeping teams together and yet encouraging a reasonable amount of rotation, the organization gets the benefits of both stable teams and of consistently spread knowledge and experience.

Shrinking Teams

As a team grows in capability, keep its workload constant but gradually reduce its size. This frees people to form more teams. When the team has too few members, merge it with another too-small team. This is a practice used by the Toyota Production System. I haven't actually used it, but it makes so much sense to me that I include it here. The other strategies I've seen for scaling up to larger workloads, like creating bigger and bigger teams, work so poorly that alternatives are worth considering.

Since I don't have experience with this practice, I'll explain by analogy. Say five people work together in a manufacturing cell. Rather than load them all equally, make sure that as many people as possible are fully engaged. The fifth person, then, might be working only 30% of the time. This is good. The team members, as they do their work, also think about how to improve their work process. They try ideas until they eliminate enough wasted effort that the fifth person is no longer needed. Trying to keep everyone looking busy obscures the fact that the team has extra resources available.

Try the same in software development. Figure out how many stories the customer needs each week. Strive to improve development until some of the team members are idle; then you're ready to shrink the team and continue.

Root-Cause Analysis

Every time a defect is found after development, eliminate the defect and its cause. The goal is not just that this one defect won't ever recur, but that the team will never make the same kind of mistake again.

In XP, this is the process for responding to a defect:

1. Write an automated system-level test that demonstrates the defect, including the desired behavior. This can be done by the customer, by customer support, or by developers.
2. Write a unit test with the smallest possible scope that also reproduces the defect.
3. Fix the system so the unit test works. This should cause the system test to pass also. If not, return to 2.
4. Once the defect is resolved, figure out why the defect was created and wasn't caught. Initiate the necessary changes to prevent this kind of defect in the future.

Taiichi Ohno has a simple exercise for this last step, the Five Whys. Ask five times why a problem occurred. So, for example,

1. Why did we miss this defect? Because we didn't know the balance could be negative overnight.
2. Why didn't we know? Because only Mrs. Crosby knows and she isn't part of the team.
3. Why isn't she part of the team? Because she is still supporting the old system and no one else knows how.
4. Why doesn't anyone else know how? Because it isn't a management priority to teach anyone.
5. Why isn't it a management priority? Because they didn't know that a $20,000 investment could have saved us $500,000.

After Five Whys, you find the people problem lying at the heart of the defect (and it's almost always a people problem). Addressing that problem and the other problems encountered along the way will give you some reassurance that you won't ever have to deal with this particular mistake again.

I've put formal regression testing, as opposed to just writing another test, in the corollary practices because most teams have too many defects to be able to invest heavily in resolving each of them. Once the defect rate is down to one a week or one a month, though, the investment is proportional and the team has practice improving in other ways. It is ready for a deeper look at its own weaknesses.

Shared Code

Anyone on the team can improve any part of the system at any time. If something is wrong with the system and fixing it is not out of scope for what I'm doing right now, I should go ahead and fix it.

One objection I've heard is that if no one person is responsible for a piece of code, then everyone will act irresponsibly. They will make expedient changes, leaving a mess for the next person who has to touch the code. The risk of this happening is why I've listed Shared Code as a corollary practice. Until the team has developed a sense of collective responsibility, no one is responsible and quality will deteriorate. People will make changes without regard for the team-wide consequences.

There are other models of teamwork besides "every man for himself." The team members can collectively assume responsibility not just for the quality of what they deliver to users but also for the pride they take in their work along the way. Pair programming helps teammates demonstrate their commitment to quality to each other and helps them normalize their expectations for what constitutes quality.

Continuous integration is another important prerequisite for collective ownership. A two-hour programming session can touch many parts of the system if there are many opportunities for improvement. Two pairs making many, widespread changes increase the chance of expensive-to-resolve incompatible changes. If the team is making lots of changes, it may want to reduce the interval between integrations to keep the cost of integration down.

Code and Tests

Maintain only the code and the tests as permanent artifacts. Generate other documents from the code and tests. Rely on social mechanisms to keep alive important history of the project.

Customers pay for the what the system does today and what the team can make the system do tomorrow. Any artifacts contributing to these two sources of value are themselves valuable. Everything else is waste.

Code and Tests is a practice that is easy to approach a little at a time. A complicated five-stage document-driven process can be lightened up a little at a time as the team acquires more skill. The better the team is at incremental design, the fewer design decisions it has to make up front. The clearer the quarterly cycle becomes at expressing the business priorities, the slimmer the requirement document needs to be.

The trend in software development has been just the opposite for decades. Ceremony interferes with the flow of value. The valuable decisions in software development are: What are we going to do? What aren't we going to do? and How are we going to do what we do? Bringing those decisions together so they can feed each other smooths the flow of value. Eliminating now-obsolete artifacts enables that improvement.

Single Code Base

There is only one code stream. You can develop in a temporary branch, but never let it live longer than a few hours.

Multiple code streams are an enormous source of waste in software development. I fix a defect in the currently deployed software. Then I have to retrofit the fix to all the other deployed versions and the active development branch. Then you find that my fix broke something you were working on and you interrupt me to fix my fix. And on and on.

There are legitimate reasons for having multiple versions of the source code active at one time. Sometimes, though, all that is at work is simple expedience, a micro-optimization taken without a view to the macro-consequences. If you have multiple code bases, put a plan in place for reducing them gradually. You can improve the build system to create several products from a single code base. You can move the variation into configuration files. Whatever you have to do, improve your process until you no longer need multiple versions of the code.

One of my clients had seven different code bases for seven different customers and it was costing them more than they could afford. Development was taking far longer than it used to. Programmers were creating far more defects than before. Programming just wasn't as fun as it had been initially. When I pointed out the costs of the multiple code bases and the impossibility of scaling such a practice, the client responded that they simply couldn't afford the work of reuniting the code. I couldn't convince the client to even try reducing from seven to six versions or adding the next customer as a variation of one of the existing versions.

Don't make more versions of your source code. Rather than add more code bases, fix the underlying design problem that is preventing you from running from a single code base. If you have a legitimate reason for having multiple versions, look at those reasons as assumptions to be challenged rather than absolutes. It might take a while to unravel deep assumptions, but that unraveling may open the door to the next round of improvement.

Daily Deployment

Put new software into production every night. Any gap between what is on a programmer's desk and what is in production is a risk. A programmer out of sync with the deployed software risks making decisions without getting accurate feedback about those decisions.

Daily deployment is a corollary practice because it has so many prerequisites. The defect rate must be at most a handful per year. The build environment must be smoothly automated. The deployment tools must be automated, including the ability to roll out incrementally and roll back in case of failure. Most importantly, the trust in the team and with customers must be highly developed.

The trend towards more frequently deployed software is clear. My instant messaging program fetches updates every few days. Large web sites change imperceptibly daily. Daily deployment is an extrapolation of this trend.

Daily deployment is a good example of a practice that points in a direction. If you can't deploy more frequently than once a year, daily deployment might seem like a pipe dream. I've seen teams that think they deploy once a year actually deploy twelve times a year—one release and eleven patches. The team is capable of rolling out small increments of functionality, but the team is embarrassed about needing to do so rather than seeing its capability as an opportunity. Twelve releases sound a lot better than eleven patches.

How do you implement daily deployment when you have projects that take weeks or months before they are usable? There are many tasks involved in a big project: restructuring the database, implementing new features, and changing the user interface. As long as you don't change the user's experience of the system, you can deploy all the rest of that work. On the last day you put the "keystone", the change to the user interface, in place.

There are many barriers to deploying frequently. Some are technical, like having too many defects or needing an inexpensive way to deploy. Some are psychological or social, like a deployment process so stressful that people don't want to go through it twice as often. Some are business-related, like not having a way of charging for more frequent releases. Whatever the barrier, working to remove it and then letting more frequent deployment come as a natural consequence will help you improve development.

Negotiated Scope Contract

Write contracts for software development that fix time, costs, and quality but call for an ongoing negotiation of the precise scope of the system. Reduce risk by signing a sequence of short contracts instead of one long one.

You can move in the direction of negotiated scope. Big, long contracts can be split in half or thirds, with the optional part to be exercised only if both parties agree. Contracts with high costs for "change requests" can be written with less scope fixed up front and lower costs for changes.

Negotiated scope contracts are a piece of software development advice. They're are a mechanism for aligning the interests of suppliers and customers to encourage communication and feedback, and to give everyone the courage to do what looks right today, not do something ineffective just because it is in the contract. They might be unwise for you at the moment for business or legal reasons. Moving in the direction of negotiated scope gives you a source of information with which to improve.

Pay-Per-Use

With pay-per-use systems, you charge for every time the system is used. Money is the ultimate feedback. Not only is it concrete, you can also spend it. Connecting money flow directly to software development provides accurate, timely information with which to drive improvement.

Lots of software is already pay-per-use. Telephone switches, electronic stock exchanges, and airline reservation systems all charge you a fee per transaction. While pay-per-use has business advantages and disadvantages, the information it generates can help improve software development.

The ultimate form of pay-per-use I've seen was in a messaging product. Users were charged per message. Each story in development was deliberately selected to encourage more messages. Support for a new handset, for instance, came with both a cost estimate and a revenue estimate. The team analyzed the usage of the system to provide feedback for the accuracy of the revenue estimates. The team used this information to optimize both cost and profitability.

Today's typical arrangement requires the customer to pay for each release of the software. Pay-per-release opposes the supplier's interests and the customer's interests. The supplier is selfishly motivated to have lots of releases, each containing the least possible functionality necessary to get the customers to pay. The customer wants fewer releases (because of the pain of upgrading), each containing lots of features. The tension between the two sets of interests reduces communication and feedback.

Even if you can't implement pay-per-use, you might be able to go to a subscription model, in which software is purchased monthly or quarterly. With the subscription model, the team at least has the retention rates (the number of customers that continue to subscribe) as a source of information about how the team is doing. An even smaller change of business model is to weight contracts more toward support fees and less toward up-front revenue.

One objection to pay-per-use is that customers want predictable costs. If the price advantage of pay-per-use is large enough, customers may not mind. A team using the information provided by pay-per-use should be able to do a more effective job than a team relying for feedback only on license revenues.

Conclusion

The primary and corollary practices are not everything you need to do to successfully develop software. They are, however, what my observations lead me to believe are the core of excellence for software development teams. If you find yourself with a problem not covered by one of the practices, that's the time to look back at the values and the principles to come up with an appropriate solution for your team.

Chapter 10

The Whole XP Team

Many people's perspectives must come into play for effective software development to occur. The XP practice Whole Team suggests that a variety of people work together in interlinking ways to make a project more effective. They have to work together as a group for each to be successful. Everyone on an XP team has linked his future in the realm of work. XP started out prescribing effective ways for programmers to behave on a project. Here are the beginnings of prescriptions for each member of an XP team.

The principle of flow suggests that more value is created in a smooth, steady stream of software than in occasional large deployments. Flow is particularly important in structuring the different kinds of work that go into software development, but it can be difficult to apply. I remember sitting in an all-day meeting planning how an organization wanted to develop software. The programmers and executives were there at the beginning of the day. Representatives of different specialities were scheduled to join the meeting throughout the day to give their perspectives on what style of development was needed.

The programmers started by talking about XP: risk management, immediate return, feedback, and why we favored activities over phases. Heads were nodding. It all made sense.

Then in came the architects. They explained that, while XP was okay for programming, if they designed the architecture in a phase at the beginning of projects everything would run much more smoothly. They were showered with the arguments for flow and how that meant that they would have to continuously refine the architecture as they went along, starting with just enough architecture to get going. They reluctantly agreed that they could do so, but it wouldn't be as good as an architecture phase.

Next came the interaction designers. They explained that, while XP was okay for programming, if they designed the interaction in a phase at the beginning of projects everything would run much more smoothly. The programmers, executives, and architects came back with all the arguments for flow. The interaction designers supposed they could continuously refine the interaction, starting with just enough interaction to get going; but it wouldn't be as good as if they could do their work at the beginning of the project.

By the time the infrastructure planners proposed that we let them make all the infrastructure decisions at the beginning of the project, the meeting was getting comical. It didn't take long to get their reluctant agreement to work incrementally.

There was no happy ending to this story. You can't be convinced against your will. None of the groups saw themselves as part of a larger whole. Under stress, they reverted to trying to do all of their work up front.

It was as if the different perspectives were roped together walking up a glacier and all they wanted to do was argue about who got to be first in line. It didn't really matter who was first. What the whole team was missing was a sense that they were roped together. Walking abreast, they could make more progress than if any one group tried to force the others to follow.

Testers

Testers on an XP team help customers choose and write automated system-level tests in advance of implementation and coach programmers on testing techniques. On XP teams much of the responsibility for catching trivial mistakes is accepted by the programmers. Test-first programming results in a suite of tests that help keep the project stable. The role of testers shifts to early in development, helping define and specify what will constitute acceptable functioning of the system before the functionality has been implemented.

In Weekly Cycle, the first thing that happens to the chosen stories is that they are turned into automated system-level tests. This is one leveraged place for strong testing skills. Customers may have a good idea of the general behavior they want to see, but testers are good at looking at "happy paths" and asking what should happen if something goes wrong. "Okay, but what if login fails three times? What should happen then?" In this role testers amplify communication. They ensure that the system-level tests succeed only when the stories are fully implemented and ready for deployment.

Once the tests for the week are written and failing, testers continue to write new tests as implementation uncovers new details that need to be specified. Testers can also work to further automate and tune tests. Finally, when a programmer gets stuck on a knotty testing problem, a tester can pair with the programmer to help solve the problem.

Interaction Designers

Interaction designers on an XP team choose overall metaphors for the system, write stories, and evaluate usage of the deployed system to find opportunities for new stories. Addressing the concerns of eventual users is a priority for the team. The tools of interaction design, such as personas and goals, help the team analyze and make sense of the world of the user, although they are no substitute for conversation with real people.

Much advice for interaction designers is based on a phasist model of development: first interaction designers figure out what the system is supposed to do, and then programmers go make it do that. Phases reduce feedback and restrict the flow of value. Mutual benefit is possible between interaction design and the rest of an XP team without separating development into phases.

On an XP team, interaction designers work with customers, helping to write and clarify stories. Interaction designers can use all their usual tools during this process. They also analyze actual usage of the system to decide what the system needs to do next. Interaction designers specify a little bit up front and continue to refine the user interface throughout the life of the project.

Architects

Architects on an XP team look for and execute large-scale refactorings, write system-level tests that stress the architecture, and implement stories. Architects apply their expertise a little bit at a time throughout the project. They direct the architecture of the project throughout its evolution. The architecture for a little system should not be the same as for a big system. While the system is little the architect makes sure the system has just the right little architecture. As the system grows, the architect makes sure the architecture keeps pace.

Making big architectural changes in small, safe steps is one of the challenges for an XP team. The principle of the alignment of authority and responsibility suggests that it is a bad idea to give one person the power to make decisions that others have to follow without having to personally live with the consequences. Architects sign up for programming tasks just like any programmer. However, they are also on the lookout for big changes that have big payoffs.

Tests can communicate architectural intent. I talked with the architect of a major credit card processor who said that in such a high-capacity environment you don't want any architecture that might get in the way. To achieve this his team had a sophisticated stress testing environment. When they wanted to improve the architecture they would first improve the stress tests until the system broke. Then they would improve the architecture just enough to run the tests.

I suggested this strategy to an architect at another company. He complained of spending all of his time writing specifications and then explaining them to developers. He was frustrated that he didn't have time to code any more. I suggested he write a testing infrastructure and then use tests instead of specifications and explanations. If he saw a hole in a design he should write a failing test to point it out. I wasn't able to convince him to try the idea, but I still think it's valuable.

Another task for architects on an XP team is partitioning systems. Partitioning isn't an up-front, once-and-for-all task, though. Rather than divide and conquer, an XP team conquers and divides. First a small team writes a small system. Then they find the natural fracture lines and divide the system into relatively independent parts for expansion. The architects help choose the most appropriate fracture lines and then follow the system as a whole, keeping the big picture in mind as the groups focus on their smaller section.

Project Managers

Project managers on an XP team facilitate communication inside the team and coordinate communication with customers, suppliers, and the rest of the organization. Project managers act as team historians, reminding the team how much progress it has made. Project managers need to be creative in packaging the project's information for presentation to executives and peers. To remain accurate, the information changes frequently; which gives project managers the challenge of communicating changes helpfully.

Planning in XP is an activity, not a phase. Project managers are responsible for keeping plans synchronized with reality. They are often in the best position to drive improvement in the planning process itself. Teams may start spending a day on planning every week; but with continual improvement, they can get better results in less time. The best teams accurately plan a week's worth of work in an hour, but achieving this efficiency requires practice.

Information flows both ways, into and out of the team. Project managers facilitate communication coming into the team from customers, sponsors, suppliers, and users. To facilitate communication, they introduce the right person on the team to the right person outside the team as needed, rather than act as a communication bottleneck. Project managers also facilitate communication within the team, increasing cohesiveness and confidence. The power gained from being an effective facilitator exceeds that of being a controller of even important information.

Product Managers

In XP, product managers write stories, pick themes and stories in the quarterly cycle, pick stories in the weekly cycle, and answer questions as implementation uncovers under-specified areas of stories. A product manager doesn't just pick a bunch of stories at the beginning of the project and then sit back. A plan in XP is an example of what *could* happen, not a prediction of what *will* happen.

When the team has overcommitted, the product manager helps the team decide priorities by analyzing the differences between actual and assumed requirements. The product manager adapts the story and theme to what is really happening now.

Stories should be sequenced for business, not technical, reasons. The goal is a working system from the first week. Product managers don't necessarily start at the beginning and work through to the end. I talked to the product manager for a planning tool. He wanted to try the editing features first. The programmers didn't think it made sense to modify information before the user could enter it in the first place. Since editing was the most valuable part of the product, the product manager defined a dummy data set that could be entered manually by the programmers. Then everyone could see what editing was like. This gave the whole team an early look at the heart of the product and gave them plenty of time to refine it.

The system should be "whole" at the end of the first weekly cycle. If you plan to process images, you should be able to process an image at the end of the first week. The product manager picks stories to make this happen.

Product managers encourage communication between customers and programmers, making sure the most important customer concerns are heard and acted on by the team. If the team is practicing Real Customer Involvement, product managers are responsible for encouraging the system to grow in a way that meets the particular needs of the customers who are picking stories as well as the market as a whole.

Executives

Executives provide an XP team with courage, confidence, and accountability. The strength of an XP team, shared progress toward shared goals, can also be a weakness. What if the team's goal doesn't align with corporate goals? What if the goal drifts because of the pressures and excitements of success? Articulating and maintaining large-scale goals is one job for executives sponsoring or overseeing XP teams.

Another job for executives sponsoring or overseeing XP teams is monitoring, encouraging, and facilitating improvement. Since the goal of XP is making outstanding software development the norm, executives have a right to see not just good software coming from the team, but continuing improvement as well.

Executives are free to ask for explanations about any aspect of an XP project. The explanations should make sense. If they don't, the executive should expect the team to reflect and provide a clear explanation.

Executives should expect honesty and clear explanations of options from the team in any decision-making process. The executive needs to keep perspective in the face of problems, focusing on the actual needs of the organization and requirements of the project even when faced with the need to cut scope. Because of frequent, open communication, when such a decision is required, the executive already has the information necessary to make an informed decision.

I trust two metrics to measure the health of XP teams. The first is the number of defects found after development. An XP team should have dramatically fewer defects in its first deployment and make rapid progress from there. Some XP teams that have been on the path of improvement for several years see only a handful of defects per year. No defect is acceptable; each is an opportunity for the team to learn and improve.

The second metric I use is the time lag between the beginning of investment in an idea and when the idea first generates revenue. Even small organizations typically find they take more than a year from investment to return. Gradually reducing the time from investment to return increases the amount and timeliness of feedback available to the whole team.

Both post-development defects and investment-to-return are indicators of team effectiveness much as a speedometer is an indicator of speed. You don't make a car go faster by grabbing the speedometer needle and moving it over. If you want to go faster, you push on the gas pedal and then look at the speedometer to see if that was effective. Similarly, while you can set goals based on metrics, your team needs to address underlying problems. Trying to "game" the numbers directly will not result in improvement of anything but the numbers and defeats the value of transparency on the project.

XP teams may not match the organization's expectations. Part of the executive's job is presenting the team positively to the rest of the organization. The team is willing to stand or fall on its own merits. The executive needs to have the courage to proceed in the face of criticism. Once the team begins deploying new functionality frequently, the bottleneck in the flow of value will shift elsewhere in the organization. The executive needs to prepare the company to see this shift in a positive light. After the constraint shifts, executives must be prepared to stand firm in the face of demands that software development change back to keep other departments from looking bad.

People evaluating XP teams should understand what an effective team looks like. This may differ from other teams they have seen. For example, talking and working go together on an XP team. The hum of conversation is a sign of health. Silence is the sound of risk piling up. Executives may need to learn new rules of thumb to understand and effectively apply their experience and perspective to XP teams.

Technical Writers

The role of technical publications on an XP team is to provide early feedback about features and to create closer relationships with users. The first part of the role comes because the technical writers on the team are the first to see features, often while they are just sketches. If the writer is sitting in the room with the rest of the team he can say, "How am I going to explain that?" Maybe there is a good way to explain it and maybe there isn't. Either way, the team as a whole learns. Explaining the system in prose and pictures is an important link in the chain that creates feedback for the team.

The second part of the role is creating closer relationships with users: helping them learn about the product, listening to their feedback, and addressing confusion with further publications or new stories. The publications can take any form: tutorials, reference manuals, technical overviews, video, and audio. Writers should listen to customers, listening for the types of misunderstandings that arise when users really use the product. Weaknesses in communication are corrected with further publications. Weaknesses in the product turn into input for the planning process. You might, for example, pick stories that address a certain kind of "user error" based on users' criticisms.

The challenge of doing technical publications with XP comes from the pace of change of an XP-developed system. Back in the old days, you would freeze the specification early in development. The writers would turn it into manuals while the programmers turned it into code. In the XP world, the whole precise specification isn't frozen until very late in the game. The better the team, the later it is willing to make big changes. This leaves technical publications always playing catch-up.

You can get close, though. This week's stories can become next week's documentation tasks, putting the completion of the documentation one week behind the completion of the stories. Once you master that, you can try to have the documentation done the same week as the stories.

What would be the perfect documentation? It would be done exactly when the features it documents are done. It would be trivial to update when it was found in need of improvement. It would be cheap. It wouldn't add any time to the basic development cycle. It would be valuable to the users. The writing of it would be valuable to the team.

The XP philosophy is to start where you are now and move towards the ideal. From where you are now, could you improve a little bit? If you are using paper manuals that add six weeks to the deployment cycle, could you go fully electronic? Could you send out paper manuals six weeks after deployment? If you already have fully electronic documentation but it's not done until two months after the features, can you figure out a way to shift the time you spend so it's done two weeks after? The same week?

XP teams should get feedback from actual usage. If the manuals are online at your site, then you can monitor usage. If users never look at a certain kind of documentation, stop writing it. You can find better ways to invest that time. If the documentation is deployed with the product and the product has usage tracking built in, ask to have documentation usage added to the tracking. This will help you provide more of what your customers value.

Users

Users on an XP team help write and pick stories and make domain decisions during development. Users are most valuable if they have broad knowledge and experience with systems similar to the one being built and if they have strong relationships with the larger user community that will use the system once it is fully deployed. Users need to keep in mind that they are speaking for an entire community. They should defer decisions with broad consequences until they can talk with others in that community, giving the team other stories to work on in the meantime.

Programmers

Programmers on an XP team estimate stories and tasks, break stories into tasks, write tests, write code to implement features, automate tedious development process, and gradually improve the design of the system. Programmers work in close technical collaboration with each other, pairing on production code, so they need to develop good social and relationship skills.

Human Resources

Two challenges have been reported for human resources when teams begin applying XP: reviews and hiring. The problem with reviews is that most reviews and raises are based on individual goals and achievements, but XP focuses on team performance. If a programmer spends half of his time pairing with others, how can you evaluate his individual performance? How much incentive does he have to help others if he will be evaluated on individual performance?

Evaluating XP team members individually need not be much different from evaluating them before applying XP. In XP, valuable employees:

- ◇ Act respectful.
- ◇ Play well with others.
- ◇ Take initiative.
- ◇ Deliver on their commitments.

Teams have solved the evaluation problem in two ways: either by continuing individual goals, reviews, and raises or by moving to team-based incentives and raises. The transparency of XP gives managers plentiful information on which to base individual evaluations. Every week each team member publicly signs up for, estimates, and accomplishes tasks directly related to work requested by the customers. The need for altruistic behavior, however, moves some teams to give raises to the team as a whole instead of to individuals. Another idea is to mix the two, with individual evaluations and raises and bonuses for excellent teamwork.

Hiring for XP teams can differ from existing hiring practices. XP teams put much more emphasis on teamwork and social skills. Given the choice between an extremely skilled loner and a competent-but-social programmer, XP teams consistently choose the more social candidate. The best interviewing technique is to have the candidate work with the team for a day. Pair programming provides an excellent test of technical and social skills.

Roles

Roles on a mature XP team aren't fixed and rigid. The goal is to have everyone contribute the best he has to offer to the team's success. At first, fixed roles can help in learning new habits, like having technical people make technical decisions and business people make business decisions. After new, mutually respectful relationships are established among the team members, fixed roles interfere with the goal of having everyone do his best. Programmers can write a story if they are in the best position to write the story. Project managers can suggest architectural improvements if they are in the best position to suggest architectural improvements.

In saying that the above roles can contribute to an XP team, I don't mean to imply that there is a simple mapping from one person to one role. A programmer may be a bit of an architect. A user may grow into a product manager. A technical writer can also test. The goal is not for people to fill abstract roles, but for each team member to contribute all he can to the team.

As the team matures, keep in mind the alignment of authority and responsibility. Everyone on the team can recommend changes, but they should be prepared to back up their concerns with action.

Chapter 11

The Theory of Constraints

Find opportunities for improvement in software development by first figuring out which problems are development problems. XP isn't intended to solve marketing, sales, or management problems. It's not that non-software bottlenecks aren't important, it's just that XP doesn't spread that thin. There may be ways to crank the knobs to 10 in other areas too, but that is outside the scope of XP. XP is a coherent body of values, principles, and practices for addressing software development problems. We need a way to look at software development as a whole.

One approach to looking at the throughput of entire systems is the Theory of Constraints. I'll illustrate the theory with an example from my own laundry room (Figure 9). My washer takes forty-five minutes to clean clothes, my dryer takes ninety minutes to dry them, and folding the clothes takes fifteen minutes.

The bottleneck in this system is drying. If I get two washers, I won't get any more clothes finished. I'll temporarily get more clothes washed,

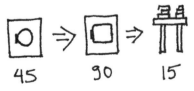

FIGURE 9. Current state of the laundry process

but then I'll have to contend with the stacks of wet clothes all over the place, and I'll probably get fewer clothes finished. If I want to get more clothes finished, I have no choice but to do something about drying.

The Theory of Constraints says that in any system there is one constraint at a time (occasionally two). To improve overall system throughput you have to first find the constraint; make sure it is working full speed; then find ways of either increasing the capacity of the constraint, offloading some of the work onto non-constraints, or eliminating the constraint entirely.

How do you find the constraint in a system? Work piles up in front of the constraint. There are not piles of dried clothes sitting waiting to be folded; there are piles of wet clothes sitting waiting to be dried.

The dryer is the constraint. To make sure it is working at full capacity, I turn on that annoying buzzer that tells me when a dryer load is finished. When I hear the buzzer, I shift a load. I don't need the buzzer on the washer because I only start a load when I shift one out of the dryer. Work is pulled through the system based on actual demand, not pushed through the system based on projected demand.

If I still need more clothes laundered, I need to increase the capacity of the drying step. This could be done by buying a bigger dryer or by speeding drying by keeping the dryer vent unclogged. I could also offload drying work by buying a new washing machine that spins clothes faster, so they don't take as long in the dryer. Or, I could take the clothes outside and hang them in the sun, as shown in Figure 10.

Now the constraint has moved either to the washer or the folding table. The Theory of Constraints says there is always a constraint. When

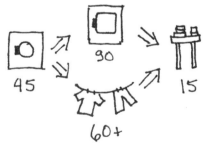

FIGURE 10. Increasing throughput by hanging clothes to dry

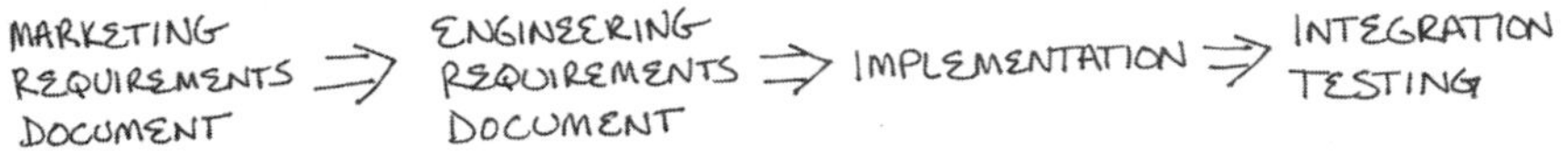

MARKETING → ENGINEERING → IMPLEMENTATION → INTEGRATION
REQUIREMENTS   REQUIREMENTS   TESTING
DOCUMENT   DOCUMENT

FIGURE 11. Waterfall process

we eliminate one constraint we create another. Micro-optimization is never enough. To improve our results we must look at the whole situation before deciding what to change.

In software, the constraints in the system need to be identified too. Figure 11 is the familiar, often ineffective, waterfall software development style.

Even if I know how long each of the steps takes I still can't identify the bottleneck. To find the bottleneck, I look for work piling up. If the ERD covers lots of features that get dropped late in implementation because there is too much to do, I suspect the implementation process. If many features are implemented, but waiting to be integrated and deployed, I suspect that the integration process is the constraint.

If integration is the constraint, I first look to make sure integration is going as smoothly as it can given its inputs and its environment. Perhaps people could be shifted from implementation to integration. I have seen one overwhelmed deployment person holding up the efforts of twenty programmers. Asking a few programmers to help with deployment would have helped overall throughput.

Once integration is working smoothly, I look for ways to offload integration work upstream, perhaps by automating tests during implementation. This might slow implementation but improve overall system throughput (more likely, it would make implementation faster, but that's a story for a different chapter).

The point made above about work being pulled through the system is true in software as well. The "push" model of development (Figure 12)

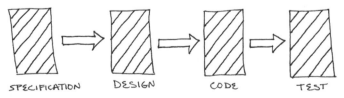

SPECIFICATION   DESIGN   CODE   TEST

FIGURE 12. Push model of development

is to pile up requirements to be done, then designs to be implemented, then code to be integrated and tested; culminating in an aptly-named big bang integration. XP uses a "pull" model (Figure 13). Stories are specified in detail immediately before they are implemented. The tests are pulled from the specifications. The programming interface is designed to match the needs of the test. The code is written to match the tests and the interface. The design is refined to match the needs of the code as written. This leads to a decision about which story to specify next. In the meantime, the rest of the stories remain on the wall until chosen for implementation.

The Theory of Constraints shares with other theories of organizational change the assumption that the whole organization is focused on overall throughput, not on micro-optimization. If everyone is trying to make sure his function is not seen as the constraint, no change will happen. If the developers say, "Yes, writing automated tests would be 'A Good Thing', but it will slow me down and I'm overloaded as it is," then nothing will change regardless of how beneficial the change would be to the organization and thus to the individuals in it. The reward system and culture need to align with overall throughput instead of individual productivity for the change to stick.

A weakness of the Theory of Constraints is that it is a model: a map, not the territory. People develop software; they are not boxes in a model. The closer an organization is to efficient but superficially cha-

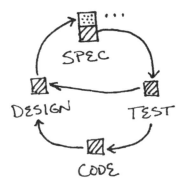

FIGURE 13. **Pull model of development**

otic communication the less accurate the mapping will be into the world of the Theory of Constraints and back again. Software development is a human process not a factory. However, the Theory of Constraints is a good way to become aware of your process. Draw your current process as a series of linked activities and look for where work piles up.

The Theory of Constraints can help find bottlenecks, but what if the bottleneck has nothing to do with software? One of my clients deploys non-safety-critical software on airplanes. Their first partner took as long as four months to deploy finished software on the planes because it would only deploy the software when the planes came in for service. My client picked a second partner who had the infrastructure to deploy new software every day, eliminating that constraint (and moving it to marketing). If the bottleneck exists outside of software development, the answer must come from outside of software development.

I am sometimes tempted to expand the scope of XP to include issues like choosing business partners. Sometimes I'm afraid that if XP doesn't cover a wide range of problems, people won't see it as important. In clearer moments, I believe that XP's value will be more apparent to business with a clear, narrow scope.

Sometimes XP can facilitate shifting the constraint out of software development completely, so XP will have ripple effects throughout an organization applying it. For example, you begin having weekly meetings where the business-focused part of the team (product managers and customers, for instance) chooses the features to be added that week. The programmers may learn to go fast enough that product marketing can't specify features fast enough. The constraint has shifted out of software development.

Here's a sad but repeated story: a development team begins applying XP, dramatically improves quality and productivity, but then is disbanded, its leaders fired and the rest of the team scattered. Why does this happen? From the Theory of Constraint perspective, the team's improved performance shifted the constraint elsewhere in the organization. The new constraint (e.g. marketing, who can't decide what they want fast enough) doesn't like the spotlight. Nobody actually cares about organizational throughput. The "source" of the turmoil, XP, is blamed and eliminated.

Executive sponsorship and strong relationships with people outside the team are crucial to applying XP, precisely because applying XP will shift the structure of work in the rest of the organization as soon as software development gets its act together. If you don't have executive sponsorship, be prepared to do a better job yourself without recognition or protection.

Chapter 12

Planning: Managing Scope

The state of a shared plan provides clues about the state of the relationship between the people affected by the plan. A plan out of touch with reality betrays an unclear, unbalanced relationship. A mutually agreed-upon plan, adjusted when necessary to reflect changing reality, suggests a respectful, mutually valuable relationship.

Planning makes goals and directions clear and explicit. Planning in XP starts with putting the current goals, assumptions, and facts on the table. With current, explicit information, you can work toward agreement about what's in scope, what's out of scope, and what to do next.

Planning in XP is like shopping for groceries. Imagine that you go into a grocery store with $100 in your pocket. Items on the shelves each have a price attached. Some items you need; others you don't; and still others you want, but they don't fit your budget. If you get to the checkout with $101 worth of food, you have to put something back. Your job while shopping is to spend your $100 wisely, buying what you need and as much of what you want as possible.

In XP, the groceries are the stories. The prices are the estimates attached to the stories. The budget is the amount of time available. The desired deployment date is usually set early in a project, so you know how much you have to spend on stories. If you have two hundred pair-hours in your pocket and you have four hundred pair-hours worth of stories in your cart, pick the most valuable set of stories adding up to two hundred pair-hours. Otherwise, everyone knows you have more in the cart than you can afford.

Part of planning is deciding what to do next out of all the possibilities. Planning is complicated because the estimates of the cost and value of stories are uncertain. The information on which you base these decisions changes. We use feedback to improve our estimates and make decisions as late as possible so they are based on the best possible information. That's why planning is a daily, weekly, and quarterly activity in XP. The plan can change to fit the facts as they emerge.

Plans are not predictions of the future. At best, they express everything you know today about what might happen tomorrow. Their uncertainty doesn't negate their value. Plans help you coordinate with other teams. Plans give you a place to start. Plans help everyone on the team make choices aligned with the team's goals.

As a young software engineer, I learned three variables by which to manage projects: speed, quality, and price. The sponsor gets to fix two of these variables and the team gets to estimate the third. If the plan is unacceptable, the negotiating starts.

This model doesn't work well in practice. Time and costs are generally set outside the project. That leaves quality as the only variable you can manipulate. Lowering the quality of your work doesn't eliminate work, it just shifts it later so delays are not clearly your responsibility. You can create the illusion of progress this way, but you pay in reduced satisfaction and damaged relationships. Satisfaction comes from doing quality work.

The variable left out of this model is scope. If we make scope explicit, then:

⋄ We have a safe way to adapt.
⋄ We have a way to negotiate.
⋄ We have a limit to ridiculous and unnecessary demands.

Plan at every timescale with these four steps:

1. List the items of work that may need to be done.
2. Estimate the items.
3. Set a budget for the planning cycle.
4. Agree on the work that needs to be done within the budget. As you negotiate, don't change the estimates or the budget.

Everyone on the team needs to be heard. Planning provides a forum in which the team acknowledges wishes, but only commits to needs.

This procedure works at the scale of a pair of programmers planning a couple of hours of test cases they want to satisfy and design they want to improve. It works at the scale of a team planning the day's activities. It works more formally at the scale of team planning a week or a quarter, where stories are the items on the list, estimation is more formal, and planning takes hours or days.

Planning is something we do together. It requires cooperation. Planning is an exercise in listening, speaking, and aligning goals for a specific time period. It is valuable input for each team member. Without planning, we are individuals with haphazard connections and effectiveness. We are a team when we plan and work in harmony.

Everyone on the team should be involved in planning. Some XP teams have the customers on the team get together privately to fight over the coming week's budget. This just shifts the zero-sum game away from the programmers so they don't have the urge to overcommit. Doing this eliminates opportunity for mutual benefit. The whole team together may be able to find a way for the seemingly divergent needs of the customers to be satisfied. If the team doesn't know all of the needs or issues involved; it can't make good choices, business or technical.

When choosing which stories to implement next, sort them several ways. The act of laying the stories out spatially provides new insight into the relationships between the stories and smooths the selection process. You could put risky stories towards the left and valuable stories towards the top. You could put all the performance tuning stories in one corner of the table and all the new functionality stories in another corner. Whenever I get lost while planning, I gather all the stories up off the table, shuffle them, and lay them out fresh.

To estimate a story, imagine, given everything you know about similar stories, how many hours or days it will take a pair to complete the story. "Complete" means ready for deployment; including all the testing, implementation, refactoring, and discussions with the users. As your knowledge of similar stories increases, your estimates will improve. Estimates are based on a reasonable pair working on the story. Some pairs might be better and others worse, but if everyone takes a turn estimating it should all average out in the end.

At first, these estimates can be wildly wrong. Estimates based on experience are more accurate. It is important to get feedback as soon as possible to improve your estimates. If you have a month to plan a project in detail, spend it on four one-week iterations developing while you improve your estimates. If you have a week to plan a project, hold five one-day iterations. Feedback cycles give you information and the experience to make accurate estimates. Gain this experience as soon as possible so your estimates improve.

This provides the items (stories) and prices (estimates). How do you establish the budget (time to completion and size of team)? Measure how many productive programmer hours you get in the average week and divide by two to account for pairing. A team with six programmers and four hours of programming a day should plan on twelve pair-hours per week. One of the objections to pairing is that pairing cuts effective programming in half. In my experience, pairs are more than twice as effective. The actual time required for me to complete tasks solo versus paired, accounting for debugging time, is more than double; so by pairing you actually come out ahead in completed, clean code. When comparing the value of pairs to individuals, you need to include both time and productivity in deployable code. The goal is valuable software development delivered on time and in budget. The numbers in the plan matter, but only in service of this goal. In planning, you need to include all the relevant numbers in your calculations.

The first edition of *Extreme Programming Explained* had a more abstract estimation model, in which stories cost one, two, or three "points". Larger stories had to be broken down before they could be planned. Once you started implementing stories, you quickly discovered how many points you typically accomplished in a week. I prefer to work with real time estimates now, making all communication as clear, direct, and transparent as possible.

There is a limit to how much work can be done in a day. Paying attention to this real limit allows you to plan effectively and deliver successfully. Saying that programmers should just accomplish twice as much doesn't work. They can gain skills and effectiveness, but they cannot get more done on demand. More time at the desk does not equal increased productivity for creative work.

Whichever units you use, hours or points, you will need to deal with the situation where actual results don't match the plan. If you are estimating in real time, modify the estimates on the yet-to-be-completed stories in the light of experience. If you are estimating in points, modify the budget for subsequent cycles. A simple way to do this, dubbed "yesterday's weather" by Martin Fowler, is to plan in any given week for exactly as much work as you actually accomplished in the previous week. Adjust the plan as soon as you are sure of new information.

Sometimes you will be in the middle of a cycle with progress slower than planned. Look for ways to realign with the plan. Have you been distracted by less important issues? Have you been lax on a practice that could help you? If no process change is going to restore the balance between plan and reality, ask the customers to choose which stories they would like to see completed first. Work on those to the exclusion of all else. The time this replanning takes will be more than repaid in increased harmony and efficiency as the team works towards the deployment date. Without the adjustment, you are working under a lie. Everyone knows it and has to hide to protect themselves. This is no way to get good software done and deployed; and it undermines team and individual confidence.

When things aren't going well is when we most need to adhere to our values and principles and modify our practices to remain as effective as possible. Inaccurate estimates are a failure of information, not of values or principles. If the numbers are wrong, fix the numbers and communicate the consequences.

Write stories on index cards and put the cards on a prominent wall. Many teams try to skip this step and go straight to a computerized version of the stories. I've never seen this work. Nobody believes stories more because they are on a computer. It is the interaction around the stories that makes them valuable. The cards are a tool. The interaction and alignment of goals, shared belief in the stories, are the valuable part. You can't automate relationships. The goal is to have a plan everyone believes in and is working to fulfill.

There is a balance of power on a project: there are people who need work done and people who do work well. They both have information necessary for believable planning. Cards on a wall is a way of practicing transparency, valuing and respecting the input of each team member.

The project manager has the task of translating the cards into whatever format is expected by the rest of the organization. He or she can also teach others to read the wall. We have nothing to hide. That's the plan, open and accessible, that reflects the kind of relationships that make for the most valuable software development.

- -

Chapter 13

Testing: Early, Often, and Automated

Defects destroy the trust required for effective software development. The customers need to be able to trust the software. The managers need to be able to trust reports of progress. The programmers need to be able to trust each other. Defects destroy this trust. Without trust, people spend much of their time defending themselves against the possibility that someone else may have made a mistake.

It is impossible to eliminate all defects, however. Increasing the mean time between failures from one month to one year seems extremely expensive, and the cost to increase it to one century, as is required for code like that flying in the space shuttle, is astronomical.

Here is the dilemma in software development: defects are expensive, but eliminating defects is also expensive. However, most defects end up costing more than it would have cost to prevent them. Defects are expensive when they occur, both the direct costs of fixing the defects and the indirect costs because of damaged relationships, lost business, and lost development time. The XP practices are aimed at communicating clearly so defects don't arise in the first place, and when they do, making sure the team uses them to learn how to avoid similar problems in the future.

There will always be defects. Unexpected circumstances will arise. In novel, unanticipated situations, the software is likely to do something the author would not have intended had he known about the situation in advance.

Acceptable defect levels vary. One goal of development is to reduce the occurrence of defects to an economically sustainable level. This level is different for different kinds of software. The world's largest web site may have a hundred software errors a second and remain economically viable because 99.99% of the pages appear correctly. Any given user experiences the web site as being reliable. The space shuttle, on the other hand, might be limited to one software-related failure per century to remain viable.

Another goal of development is to reduce the occurrence of defects to a level where trust can reasonably grow on the team. Investment in defect reduction makes sense as an investment in teamwork. Mistakes introduced by one programmer make it harder for everyone else to do their work. Every mistake by one team member that affects another costs the team time, energy, and trust. Good work and good teamwork build morale and confidence. If you can respect and trust your colleagues, you can be more productive and enjoy your work more. Hiding errors to protect yourself, while sometimes seemingly necessary, is a tremendous waste of time and energy. Trust energizes participants. We feel good when things work smoothly. We need to be safe to experiment and make mistakes. We need testing to bring accountability to our experimentation so that we can be sure we are doing no harm.

Until recently, most teams have chosen to live with defects. Having essentially defect-free code, code in which you have a defect a month or a defect a year, has been considered impossible. Even cutting defect rates in half seemed to be too expensive, both in dollars and in schedule time. Many of the social practices in XP, like pair programming, tend to reduce defects. Testing in XP is a technical activity that directly addresses defects. XP applies two principles to increase the cost-effectiveness of testing: double-checking and the Defect Cost Increase.

If you add a column of numbers one way, there are many errors that could cause your sum to be wrong. Add the numbers two different ways, say from the top and then from the bottom, and if you get the same answer both ways it is very likely to be the right answer. Your chances of making two precisely offsetting errors are small.

Software testing is double-checking. You say what you want a computation to do once when you write a test. You say it quite differently when you implement the computation. If the two expressions of the computation match, the code and the tests are in harmony and likely to be correct.

Defect Cost Increase (DCI) is the second principle applied in XP to increase the cost-effectiveness of testing. DCI is one of the few empirically verified truths about software development: the sooner you find a defect, the cheaper it is to fix. If you find a defect after a decade of deployment you'll have to reconstruct a lot of history and context to figure out what the code was supposed to do in the first place, which of those assumptions are in error, and what should be fixed so the rest of the (presumably correct) program remains undisturbed. Catch the same defect the minute it is created and the cost to fix it will be minimal.

DCI implies that software development styles with long feedback loops (Figure 14) will be expensive and have many residual defects. The budget for finding and fixing defects is limited. The more finding and fixing defects costs, the more defects will remain in deployed code.

XP uses DCI in reverse to reduce both the cost of fixing defects and the number of deployed defects. By bringing automated testing into the inner loop of programming (Figure 15), XP attempts to fix defects sooner and more cheaply. This gives XP teams a chance to inexpensively develop software with very few defects by the standards of their contemporaries.

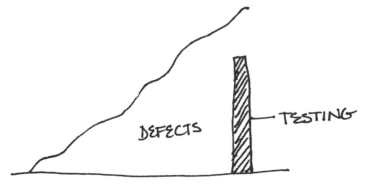

FIGURE 14. Late, expensive testing leaves many defects

FIGURE 15. Frequent testing reduces costs and defects

There are several implications to more frequent testing. One is that the same people who make the mistakes have to write the tests. If the time interval between creating and detecting a defect is months, it makes perfect sense for those two activities to belong to different people. If the gap is minutes, the cost of communicating expectations between two people would be prohibitive, even with a tester dedicated to each programmer. At some point the cost of coordination overwhelms the value gained by further shortening the gap unless you have programmers write tests.

If programmers write tests, there may still be the need for another perspective on the system. A programmer or even a pair bring to their code and tests a singular point of view on the functioning of the system, losing some of the value of double-checking. Double-checking works best when two distinct thought processes arrive at the same answer. That's why it is dangerous to copy the results of a calculation as its expected value. You've only thought it through once. It's much better to calculate an example by hand to get a second perspective.

To gain the full benefits of double-checking, in XP there are two sets of tests: one set is written from the perspective of the programmers, testing the system's components exhaustively, and another set is written from the perspective of customers or users, testing the operation of the system as whole. These tests double-check each other. If the programmers' tests are perfect, the customer tests won't catch any errors.

The immediacy of testing in XP also implies that tests must be automated. I've read involved debates about automated versus manual testing. In XP, there is no contest. Over time, by improving the design and customizing the development tools, the team reduces the cost of automating tests to the point that all testing is automated. Automated tests break the stress cycle (Figure 16).

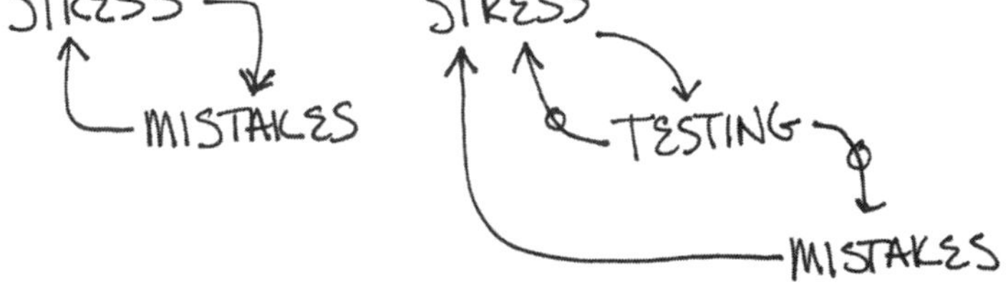

FIGURE 16. The stress cycle

With manual testing, the more stressed the team, the more mistakes the team members make in both coding and testing. With automated testing, running the tests themselves is a stress-reliever. The more stressed the team, the more tests it runs. The tests also reduce the number of errors that escape detection by the programmers.

Beta testing is a symptom of weak testing practices and poor communication with customers. However, during the transition to earlier and more frequent testing, it is wise to leave current testing practices in place. The team's goal is to eliminate all post-development testing and shift testing resources to more highly leveraged parts of the development lifecycle. If there are forms of testing, like stress and load testing, that find defects after development is "complete," bring them into the development cycle. Run load and stress tests continuously and automatically.

Static verification is a valid form of double-checking, particularly for defects that are hard to reproduce dynamically. For static checking to be most valuable it must become faster, part of the inner loop of development. Static checkers should provide feedback in seconds based on changes to a program, much as incremental compilers do now. Even in its current state, where statically verifying a substantial program can take days, it can still be valuable for providing confidence in the concurrency properties of a program. Like other tests, write static verification statements a little at a time, as the program demonstrates the need for double-checking.

DCI tells us to put testing near coding, but it doesn't say exactly when to test. Testing after implementation has the advantage that it makes sense. After all, you can't check the tolerances of a physical part you haven't yet made. This is where the physical metaphor behind the word "testing" is misleading. Because software is a virtual world, "testing" before or after makes equal sense. You can write code to fit a mold or a mold to fit code. You can do whichever creates the most benefit. In the end you put the two together and see if they match (Figure 17).

Code and tests can be written in either order. In XP, when possible, tests are written in advance of implementation. There are several advantages to writing the tests first. Folk wisdom in software development teaches that interfaces shouldn't be unduly influenced by implementations. Writing a test first is a concrete way to achieve this separation. Tests also serve the human need for certainty. When I have written all the tests that I can imagine could possibly break and they all pass, I'm certain my

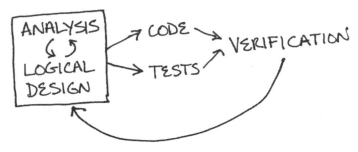

FIGURE 17. Code and test in either order

code is correct. Other tests I can't yet imagine might break, but at least I can point to what the system actually does as demonstrated by the tests.

Tests can provide a measure of progress. If I have ten tests broken and I fix one, then I've made progress. That said, I try to have only one broken test at a time. If I am programming test-first, I write one failing test, make it work, and then write the next failing test. My experience with getting the first test to work often informs my writing of the second. If I write tests based on unvalidated assumptions, I have to modify them all when the assumptions turn out to be wrong. System-level tests give me a sense of certainty that the whole system is working at the end of the week.

In XP, testing is as important as programming. Writing and running the tests gives the team a chance to do work it can be proud of. Running tests gives the team a valid basis for confidence as it moves quickly in unanticipated directions. Tests contribute value to development by strengthening the trust relationships within the team and with customers.

Chapter 14

Designing:
The Value of Time

Incremental design is a way to deliver functionality early and continue delivering functionality weekly for the life of the project. XP pushes incrementalism of design to its limit, suggesting that projects run more smoothly if design is part of daily business. This chapter explores the technical, economic, and human reasons for embracing incremental design.

Permaculture is a philosophy and practice of sustainable living in a balanced ecosystem. As in Permaculture, I think of design as a system of beneficially related elements. Each word in this definition is loaded with meaning. "Elements" suggests that systems can't be comprehended only as wholes. "Related" suggests that the elements in a design don't stand alone but rather come together in relation to each other. These relationships, along with the decomposition of a design into elements, are what the designer manipulates, consciously or unconsciously, for good or ill. "Beneficially" suggests that the relationships can strengthen the elements, making each more powerful than it would be alone and making the system something more than what would be suggested by examining the elements in isolation.

Design is what makes software so valuable. Unlike the physical world, in software we can endlessly replicate our elements at no cost. When we create new, more beneficial relationships between elements, we can spread these relationships to all existing elements. Software is a leverage game. One good idea can save millions of dollars in costs and create many millions of dollars in revenue.

Unfortunately, design in software has been shackled by metaphors from physical design activities. When you have a skyscraper fifty stories high, you can't decide to take it up another fifty stories because you've already rented all the space. There is no way to jack up a huge building and replace the foundation with something stronger.

The equivalent transformation is daily business in software. A distributed system might use remote procedure calls as its initial communication technology. As experience with the system grows, the team can see how to improve the system by moving to CORBA. A year later the team replaces CORBA with a message queue. At every stage of this process the system is running. Every stage of the process provides the experience to get to the next stage. It is as if we started with a dog house and, by gradually replacing pieces, ended up with a skyscraper, all the while continuously occupying the structure. This is absurd in the physical world but it's a sensible, low-risk way to develop software.

In the physical world the individual transformations cost too much for incremental design to work well. The intermediate stages have too little value or the changes are too costly (pieces get destroyed and are expensive to duplicate in the rebuilding process). Still, as *How Buildings Learn* by Stewart Brand documents, even physical structures undergo incremental design and construction, with the experience of the existing structure informing the next stage of design in ways that speculation cannot.

Part of what makes incremental design valuable in software is that we are often writing applications for the first time. Even if this is the umpteenth variation on a theme, there is always a better way to design the software. Because design has leverage and because design ideas improve with experience, patience is one of the most valuable skills a software designer can possess. There is an art to designing just enough to get feedback, and then using that feedback to improve the design enough to get the next round of feedback.

One common metaphor for software is building construction. For example, Steve McConnell in *Code Complete* pushes the software construction metaphor. Beth Andres-Beck, Smith College theater student, has pointed out the fundamental flaw in the metaphor: it is extremely difficult to reverse progress in the construction world. One day you can make changes to the floor plan by moving around pegs and string for free. Two days later, after the foundation has been poured, the same change costs you $10,000. This asymmetry of costs shapes the activities and their relationships in construction.

In software, however, reversing a day's work is trivial. All you ever lose is that day's work. Given this radical difference, the sequence of activities appropriate in construction are not appropriate for software. The question is not *whether* to design, but *when* to design.

McConnell writes, "In ten years the pendulum has swung from 'design everything' to 'design nothing.' But the alternative to BDUF [Big Design Up Front] isn't no design up front, it's a Little Design Up Front (LDUF) or Enough Design Up Front (ENUF)." This is a straw-man argument. The alternative to designing before implementing is designing after implementing. Some design up-front is necessary, but just enough to get the initial implementation. Further design takes place once the implementation is in place and the real constraints on the design are obvious. Far from "design nothing," the XP strategy is "design always."

The following graphs help you visualize for yourself when you should design. The vertical axis of the graph is the quality of the design. There is a horizontal line for the minimum quality of the design necessary for success. Software design is curious in that there are usually many designs that are good enough for the software to be successful. Design quality doesn't ensure success, but design failure can ensure failure.

Each graph will have three points, one for how you would design "by instinct", one for how you would design if you thought about the design really hard, and one for how you would design in the light of experience. The relationship of the three points and the location of the minimal design threshold will suggest whether designing up front is even an option for you, or whether you would be better off with incremental design.

Figure 18 is a graph where purely instinctive design is sufficient. Any old design will do. You can go ahead and design today and be successful.

Figure 19 is a scenario in which the question of when to design isn't as clear. Careful thought would lead to a good enough answer, but experience would lead to a better answer. You don't have the option of not designing at all, because unconscious design will lead to failure. Should you make the bulk of your investment in design now, or wait until you have some experience?

Figure 20 is a case in which incremental design is inevitable. No amount of thought without experience will result in a design that is

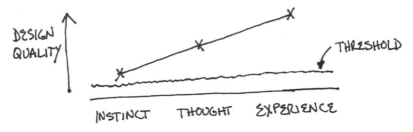

FIGURE 18. Any old design will do

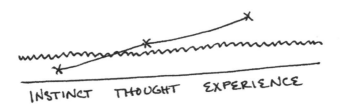

FIGURE 19. Some design thought or experience is necessary

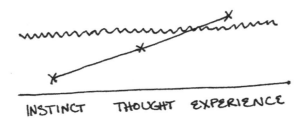

FIGURE 20. No amount of pure thought will suffice

good enough. Only experience will result in enough understanding to produce a good enough design.

One factor to take into consideration in deciding when to design is the value available through the different strategies. If pure thought creates most of the value without feedback (Figure 21), designing sooner makes more sense. If experience creates most of the value (Figure 22), designing just enough today to get going and then designing mostly in the light of experience makes more sense.

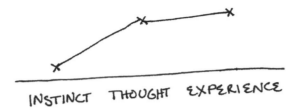

FIGURE 21. Experience doesn't help

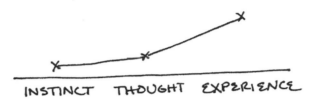

FIGURE 22. Lots to learn from experience

Another factor in deciding when to design is the cost. If you design early, the initial cost of the design is simply the time you spend. Overall costs may be high if you make many mistakes that have to be repaired or worked around for the life of the project. The cost of designing based on experience is the time for the bare-bones initial design, which is lower than that of designing up front, plus the cost of retrofitting later design decisions into running code and live data. Many XP practices are intended to lower the cost of ongoing design.

A particularly important design problem is the design of databases. Pramod Sadalage of ThoughtWorks came up with an elegant incremental database design strategy:

⬦ Start with an empty database.
⬦ Add all tables and columns with automated scripts that also migrate any existing data as necessary.
⬦ Sequentially number the scripts so a database at any earlier stage can be brought up to any later stage by running the scripts.

A particular version of the code expects a particular version of the database design. Deploying a new version of the system involves rolling out the new code and running any design/migration scripts. To reduce downtime, deployments should be kept small and frequent.

The most powerful design heuristic I know is Once and Only Once: data, structure, or logic should exist in only one place in the system. I discover the need for design investment by spotting duplication. I work with the design until I can find a way to unify the separate expressions. Patterns are the common targets of these design improvements, structures of code that generally do not require duplication. Duplication is bad because it implies that to make one conceptual change you have to change code in several places. Code without duplication has the property that one conceptual change requires one change of code. If your code has this property, continuing changes remain inexpensive.

The arguments against incremental design come down to "we can't" and "we won't." "Can't" is addressable by learning the skills necessary to design in the context of running code and data. "Won't" is a bit tougher. I've certainly worked on systems when I knew about many potential design improvements but I never invested the time to realize them in the system. Most often, I didn't improve the design because I was focused too narrowly on the problem of adding one more feature to the system. I didn't try to balance the whole team's productivity with today's task. I didn't think about how bad I felt jamming one more feature in where it didn't belong. I didn't think about how much motivation and satisfaction there is in doing a really good job.

If you are confronted with a big ball of mud, you can still begin improving the design. Begin lighting the lamps where you walk. As you modify code, clean up a little. Resist the temptation to take your design improvements too far afield. Make a habit of improving the design that affects you today. Make a public list of bigger improvements that need to be tackled over time. Soon you'll find that the code you change all the time is pretty well designed. It'll be a surprise when you run into an untouched part of the system that is designed the old way.

Sometimes the team can't make a design improvement in a week and still deliver new functionality. Part of incremental design is figuring out how to stage design improvements. Take the example that led off this chapter, moving from remote procedure calls to CORBA. Even with careful design originally, some assumptions that you are using remote procedure calls will leak out into code that is unrelated to communication. As you touch the existing code, concentrate those assumptions in as few places as possible. Eventually, the job of putting in the new communication protocol will fit into a week.

Such long-running changes may seem to cost more than stopping development and making the change all at once. Designing software is not done for its own sake in XP. Design is in service of a trust relationship between technical and business people. Weekly delivery of requested functionality is the cornerstone of that relationship. It doesn't matter what the theoretical best way to design might be. The convenience of the designers is lower on the priority list than maintaining the diverse relationships that create value within the team.

In summary, the shift to XP-style design is a shift in the timing of design decisions. Design is deferred until it can be made in the light of experience and the decisions can be used immediately. This allows the team to:

- ✧ Deploy software sooner.
- ✧ Make decisions with certainty.
- ✧ Avoid living with bad decisions.
- ✧ Maintain the pace of development as the original design assumptions are superseded.

The price of this strategy is that it requires the discipline to continue investing in design throughout the life of the project and to make large changes in small steps, so as to maintain the flow of valuable new functionality.

Simplicity

XP teams prefer simple solutions where possible. Here are four criteria used to evaluate the simplicity of a design:

1. *Appropriate for the intended audience.* It doesn't matter how brilliant and elegant a piece of design is; if the people who need to work with it don't understand it, it isn't simple for them.
2. *Communicative.* Every idea that needs to be communicated is represented in the system. Like words in a vocabulary, the elements of the system communicate to future readers.

3. *Factored.* Duplication of logic or structure makes code hard to understand and modify.
4. *Minimal.* Within the above three constraints, the system should have the fewest elements possible. Fewer elements means less to test, document, and communicate.

Projects that move toward simplicity improve both the humanity and productivity of their software development.

Chapter 15

Scaling XP

People often ask how XP scales. One hundred people can't plan their work in detail in a single meeting once a week. One hundred people can work together in a spirit of communication, feedback, simplicity, courage, and respect. Creating and maintaining a community of one hundred is a much different job than creating and maintaining a community of twelve, but it is done all the time.

The number of people on a project is not the only measure of scale for software development. Software development scales along many dimensions:

- Number of people
- Investment
- Size of the entire organization
- Time
- Problem complexity
- Solution complexity
- Consequence of failure

Number of People

This is the dimension most people seem to mean when they talk about scaling. Every medium-sized company I've visited has fond memories of how things used to be. Problems would just get solved. At some point they realized that the way problems were solved when there were two programmers no longer worked. Their solutions "didn't scale." While it is true that fifty developers can't act like two, the rigid controls and sign-offs frequently instituted aren't the only solution.

When faced with a big problem I work in three steps:

1. Turn the problem into smaller problems.
2. Apply simple solutions.
3. Apply complex solutions if any problem is left.

Following this, when faced with the apparent need for a large team, perhaps the problem really could be solved by a small team. I've seen organizations grow from fifty to three hundred and make plans to grow to two thousand, adding to their problems and losing overall throughput every step of the way. Addicted to scaling in number of employees, these organizations don't seem to want to believe that their problems would be better solved by those fifty original developers.

If just using a smaller team doesn't work, turn the big programming problem into several smaller problems, each solvable by a small team. First solve a small part of the problem with a small team. Then divide the system along its natural fracture lines and begin working on it with a few teams. Partitioning introduces the risk that the pieces won't fit on integration, so integrate frequently to reconcile differing assumptions between teams. This is a conquer-and-divide strategy instead of a divide-and-conquer strategy. Sabre Airline Solutions, profiled in the next chapter, uses this strategy extensively.

The goal of conquer-and-divide is to have teams that can each be managed as if they are the only team to limit coordination costs. Even so, the whole system needs to be integrated frequently. The occasional exceptions to this illusion of independence are managed as exceptions. If the exceptions become the norm and the teams have to spend too much time coordinating, look to the system to see if there are ways of restructuring it to return the teams to independence. Only if this fails is the overhead of large-project management appropriate.

In summary, faced with the apparent need for a large team, first ask if a small team can solve the problem. If that doesn't work, begin the project with a small team, then split the work among autonomous teams.

Investment

I'm often asked how to account for large investments in XP projects. For example, I've been asked several times whether XP-style development is an expense or a capital investment. Companies that like to expense development can justify XP as ongoing maintenance to a deployed program. Companies that account for most software development as a capital investment can use a quarterly or annual cycle to approve large amounts of development aimed at specific problems, even if the precise scope of the projects is not specified in detail in advance.

The problem lies in how accounting handles software development, not in XP itself. Blindly applying accounting models from the world of factories and widgets to an activity as different as software development inevitably creates distortions in the accounts. There is interesting work to be done outside the scope of XP in rethinking a mutually beneficial relationship between accounting and software development.

If you are starting large-scale software development XP-style, find an ally in finance early on to help you navigate these issues. Each company seems to account for software a little differently.

Size of Organization

How do you apply XP in part of an organization, when most of the organization isn't changing? While the team should quickly begin to create both more and more accurate information, forcing that information on unwilling listeners creates enemies that the team needs as friends. The goal is neither to hide the new workings of the team nor to force others to change. Be sure to maintain communication with the rest of the organization in the forms they are accustomed to.

This is an area where an XP team can benefit from a skilled project manager. If the big monthly staff meeting expects slides in a certain format, then that's exactly what the XP project manager prepares. The project manager presents the information in a form the organization can absorb. The story cards on the wall are still "the truth". Anyone who wants to learn to read them is welcome to come in, look at them, and ask questions. The project manager makes sure that the organization's expectations are met. This can be a challenge since what is going on inside the XP team is so different from what goes on inside other teams. Respect the others in the organization. Don't push your new-found knowledge and power on others for your own benefit.

Meeting organizations' expectations and at the same time maintaining what is good about XP sometimes requires creativity. At one client, each project was required to prepare a detailed quarterly plan. This seemed to be incompatible with XP and negotiating scope weekly. The boss's boss, however, was wise enough to discover the purpose of the quarterly plan and find out when it would be read. The plans were only read at a quarterly executive review at the end of the quarter. The plans were compared with what actually happened to see if the teams had acted responsibly.

On the XP team, the project manager came around every Friday and asked each team member what he had done that week. She entered this information in the quarterly plan format. At the quarterly review, the team's plan was observed to contain the most precise estimates in the organization.

No one was trying to lie with this process. The whole thing took place above board. The whole management chain knew what was happening. The team satisfied the letter of the organization's expectations by being in the right format and it satisfied the spirit of the quarterly plan by making sure it spent its time responsibly.

Time

Long-running XP projects work well because the tests prevent many of the common maintenance mistakes and tell the story of the development process. The simplest case of scaling in time is if the team maintains continuity throughout the project. Then automated testing and incremental design serve to keep the system alive and capable of further growth. A team I coached ten years ago using these techniques has been steadily adding functionality ever since. Defects are rare. Progress is unspectacular but steady. Progress doesn't need to be spectacular to grow a big, sophisticated system in ten years, even with a small team.

Projects that start and stop frequently, with the team scattered at each shutdown, are more difficult to maintain over time. In this case, XP teams often write a "Rosetta Stone" document before shutting down the project. This brief guide to future maintainers tells how to run the build-and-test process and points to interesting starting places from which to learn the system. The tests included in the build prevent maintainers from falling into pits while they learn their way around the system.

Problem Complexity

XP is ideally suited to projects requiring the close cooperation of specialists. One challenge at the beginning of such projects is getting everyone to work in concert while learning a bit about each others' specialities. For example, once I worked on a life insurance project. The actuary was patient with me as I began to learn enough actuarial math to pair with him. After a month, I was catching stupid mistakes. After several months, I was even helpful sometimes. I never became an actuary, but the resulting system (and team) was much stronger than if the actuary worked on his little corner of the system while I worked alone on the user interface.

Solution Complexity

Sometimes systems grow big and complicated, out of proportion to the problem they solve. The challenge is to stop making the problem worse. It is difficult for a struggling team to keep going when every defect fixed creates three more. XP can help.

One client began by getting the build process under control. The team improved the build so instead of taking 24 hours on a dedicated machine with lots of manual intervention, the build took an hour and could run completely automatically on any machine. Then, the team instituted stories and a story board so everyone knew who was working on what and how long they were taking. After two years of steady improvement the team reduced costs 60%, going from seventy engineers to twenty; reduced the time to fix defects 66%; and reduced the time to release for major and minor point releases by 75%, from ten weeks to two weeks. Once the team had stopped digging itself in deeper, it began to climb out by eliminating excess complexity while also fixing defects.

The XP strategy for dealing with excess complexity is always the same: chip away at the complexity while continuing to deliver. Brighten the corner where you are. If you are fixing a defect in an area, clean up while you are there. One objection is that this "extra" cleanup takes too long. The team is likely wasting time on interruptions to fix defects. Cleaning up helps reduce the overhead of work. Visible planning can make it easier for everyone to see where the time is already going so it is easier to accept the estimates necessary to do the job right.

Consequences of Failure

How do you use XP in a safety- or security-critical project? Some of the rules change because the number one value becomes safety or security. As a hospital software team I met put it, "If we make a mistake, babies die." More than XP is needed in life-critical situations.

A system isn't certifiably secure unless it has been built with a set of security principles in mind and has been audited by a security expert. While compatible with XP, these practices have to be incorporated into the team's daily work. For example, refactorings have to preserve the security of the system as well as its functionality.

Avionics and medical systems are audited before they are allowed to be deployed. XP's principle of flow suggests that auditing should not be a phase at the end of a project. Auditing should happen early and often. The instructions to auditors such as DO-178B explicitly allow software development lifecycles other than a strict waterfall. Here is an example from the Food and Drug Adminstration's "Guidance for FDA Reviewers and Industry Guidance for the Content of Premarket Submissions for Software Contained in Medical Devices":

> "There are a variety of life cycle models, such as: waterfall, spiral, evolutionary, incremental, top-down functional decomposition (or stepwise refinement), formal transformation, etc. Medical device software may be produced using any of these or other models, as long as adequate risk management activities and feedback processes are incorporated into the model selected."

Building an ongoing relationship with your auditor improves your chances of a successful audit.

Traceability, the ability to link what has changed in a system to why it changed, is built into XP, although the information isn't routinely recorded. The only change to implement traceability is to make a physical record of this information. If I am changing *this* line of code, it is because I wrote *that* test which is a part of *that* system-level test which came from *that* story which was scheduled May 24 and was ready to deploy on May 28. Your auditor will tell you what format to use in saving this information.

Conclusion

With awareness and appropriate adaptations, XP does scale. Some problems can be simplified to be easily handled by a small XP team. For others, XP must be augmented. The basic values and principles apply at all scales. The practices can be modified to suit your situation.

Chapter 16

Interview

The following is an interview with Brad Jensen, Senior Vice President, Airline Products Development, Sabre Airline Solutions.

Q: Why did you start using XP?

A: I took the job of bringing thirteen different product teams into one organization with one architecture and one look-and-feel. XP was part of my strategy. I came in and said, "The process is XP!"

Q: How many people are in your organization?

A: We have three hundred people in Airline Products Development: 240 developers, twenty-five in management and clerical, and thirty-five in testing and configuration management.

Q: How did you bring XP in?

A: Each of the thirteen product groups got a week of training from Object Mentor. Thirteen groups in thirteen weeks. We followed that up with coaching as the teams began using XP.

   If I had it to do again; I would start with one team, make sure they really "got" XP, then have them teach the next team.

Q: Do you use all of XP?

A: I have a dial in my head. For projects that fit XP, we do everything. The perfect XP project is greenfield development in Java with a motivated team. If we have to extend legacy C++ code, we have to embed XP in a more waterfall-ish project. We do more requirements and design work up front. And, we have a formal testing phase before we deploy to our customers.

The legacy projects can't keep the design simple because the design isn't simple to begin with. Because of the design complexity they can't write enough tests, and so there are too many bugs. Also, they have a hard time refactoring because of the lack of refactoring tools in C++. That's what leads to the waterfall phases at the beginning and end of the projects.

Q: What benefits have you seen from XP?

A: The pure XP projects have very few defects. We have one project that hasn't had a single defect in the two years it's been in use. The legacy XP projects have very competitive defect rates, one to two defects per thousand lines of code. The Bangalore SPIN, consisting of ten CMM level-five organizations, reports an average of eight defects per thousand lines of code. Productivity is also up, 40% on one project where we can compare XP and pre-XP development directly.

Q: XP can't have been easy for you.

A: No. At first, a third of the people are skeptical, a third buy in quickly, and a third wait and see. Eventually, 80–90% buy in, 10–20% use XP grudgingly, and 3–5% never buy in. If programmers won't pair or if they insist on owning code, have the courage to fire them. The rest of the team will bail you out.

Q: Tell me about your on-site customers.

A: A lot rides on the customer. Our customers come from our product management organization. Each team has a customer who sits in the same open space with the rest of the team. One product might have one hundred airlines as customers, so it's the product manager's job to represent all of the airlines' interests. The product managers gather requirements at users conferences, customer forums, and design councils. The design councils are most valuable. Once a year, we invite a few of the best customers for a product to come in and tell us what they want to see next. We get a year or two worth of stories at one of these design councils. We have senior developers sit in on these meetings, but it's the product manager who has final say on features.

The use of on-site customers is one of the most valuable parts of XP, but it also causes the most problems. It's great to be able to manage scope. It's great to be able to know a quarter of the way through a schedule whether you are going to make it. Without careful watching, though, scope management can turn into scope creep.

Some of our customers are great. They write good stories. They write acceptance test criteria. They help testers write acceptance tests. Some of the customers aren't so good. They want to write high-level stories, but they aren't interested in writing acceptance test criteria. In those cases, we have some very experienced developers who know a lot about the domain fill in. We've had a couple of cases where customers have tried to game the system by concealing requirements to keep the estimates down, then expecting to get the whole feature they imagine when the time comes.

Q: What advice do you have for other executives who are considering XP?

A: Definitely use XP. Plan by features. The items in the plan should be features that customers care about. Plan releases once a quarter. Plan iterations more frequently. We have two-week iterations. Make the iterations absolutely fixed. Have the customers sit with the team. Put the team in an open space. If you have to embed XP in waterfall-style development, you'll still get plenty of benefit.

Section 2

Philosophy of XP

Now that you have seen how to apply XP, here is how I see some of the ideas from other domains that connect to XP. Some of the ideas influenced XP directly; others just provide clear parallels between XP and other disciplines.

People who understand one of these other ideas, quickly grasp XP and see how the parts fit together. I spoke about XP to a group that included a very skeptical chief financial officer. In the afternoon, though, I saw a light go on for him. "This is just lean manufacturing as applied to software! I went through the shift to lean manufacturing at my last job. Now what you're saying makes sense."

Parallels with other disciplines have to be applied with care. What works on the manufacturing floor may not work in the programming room and vice versa. However, other disciplines have been working on difficult people problems, like encouraging organizational change, for decades. Understanding the lessons they have learned can help accelerate application of XP.

Chapter 17

Creation Story

Ideas that catch on have associated with them the story of how they began. These stories serve to anchor the ideas, to place them in a context from which they can be more easily understood by listeners. Here is my story of the beginning of XP.

It all started with a phone call. Would I please come have a look at the performance of a payroll system Chrysler was putting together? I had written and lectured on Smalltalk performance tuning, so I wasn't surprised to get such a call. I was a bit surprised at the answers to some of my screening questions. One in particular caught my ear:

"Do you have tests so I can be sure I don't break anything with the changes I make?"

"We aren't actually computing the right answers yet."

If I don't have to compute the right answers I can make a system go as fast as you want. I had done enough consulting to smell a bigger problem than merely performance tuning. Since I was curious, I decided to go.

I arrived on Shrove Tuesday, 1996 (around Easter). I can remember the date so precisely because the team and I had paczkis (pronounced "punchkeys"), a Polish jelly donut that is only baked on Shrove Tuesday.

I quickly spotted the signs of a project in trouble:

⋄ They had been two months away from going into production for five months.
⋄ People looked to see who was listening before answering my questions, a sign that they were protecting themselves from their teammates.
⋄ People were obviously tired and snappish.

As so often happens in consulting, the client already knew the answer. Part of my job as a consultant is to find the person with the knowledge and convey that knowledge to the person with the power. Over coffee the first morning, someone said, "If only we could wipe the hard disks, we could do this project." Everyone laughed nervously at the thought of throwing away all the code when they were only two months from deployment.

Two days later I was in a meeting with the CIO of Chrysler. I gave her three options: continue the current course and never really be sure when the software would be ready to deploy, cancel the project outright and lose all the expertise, or start over from scratch with a smaller team. She chose to start over with my involvement.

Successfully making a big change requires many components. Luck is one of them. When I got home I had an email from Ron Jeffries saying, "I need a job. Can you call me at 810.555.1234."

I called and said, "Please tell me 810 is a Detroit area code."

"Ann Arbor, but that's close enough."

That is how Ron became the first full-time XP coach.

Martin Fowler had been consulting with the project on analysis issues. I grabbed onto him to help with analysis and testing, knowing he would keep a level head even when we were trying new software development ideas. Finally, I had management support and a team willing to stick with a development style that would be uncomfortable at first.

Two weeks later I was back to kick off the project. I decided the first thing to do was to interview each member of the (shrunken) team. I wanted to know what they thought they could do to help. I started with Bob Coe, the project manager. After the initial chat, he asked, "So, how is the project going to work?"

This was the question I had been preparing for but dreading, because I didn't know exactly what I was going to say. I launched in. "We'll have these uh...uh... three-week uh...uh... iterations. In each iteration we'll implement some uh...uh... stories, which Marie [our payroll expert] will pick. We'll estimate the stories and figure out how many can fit into each iteration. We'll count the iterations and that will give us the length of the whole schedule."

"Sounds like that should work."

At the next interview, I said, "So we have these three-week iterations, each of which contains some stories. We'll make sure we have the stories in the uh...uh... first iteration so we can print one real paycheck correctly." And on and on through the day, each time becoming more comfortable with the project structure and each time adding a little more detail.

My goal in laying out the project style was to take everything I knew to be valuable about software engineering and turn the dials to 10. We would do everything that was absolutely necessary as intensely as we could imagine and we would ignore everything else. If it turned out we needed to do more, we would add that in later.

At the end of the day, I had laid out the basics of XP: an always-deployable system to which features, chosen by the customer, are added and automatically tested on a fixed heartbeat. It took experience to find out that what I thought was 10 on the dial was actually only 8 or 6.

I say "basics" because the team there did the work of applying those abstract concepts to a real project. There were procedures to work out, tools to write, skills to learn, and relationships to create and deepen. I gave them a vision of how to develop software differently. They actually developed the software that way and better.

Our first task was to estimate how long the project would take to complete. The team wrote and estimated stories. We had a day-long planning meeting at which we reviewed all the stories. Our customer picked the minimal functionality for a first deployment. Then we added up the estimates and presented the date to top managers from IT and the sponsoring organization. At the end of the day one of the programmers told me, "This is the first estimate I've ever seen that I actually believed." Then the team started implementing stories, three weeks at a time.

The team was humming and I was overly confident. I was sure we could always deliver on time by negotiating scope. However, there are no guarantees in software development. One incident in particular sticks in my mind. I was absolutely certain that by dividing the system into features and giving control of the features to the customer, our software would always be deployed on time. I had bet a bundle on getting our system into production on time (January 1997). Come the middle of November it was clear that we weren't going to make it. We were calculating the payroll numbers well enough, but they weren't showing up correctly in the output files. Our tests only went as far as the numbers. There was more work to be done to correctly export the results. (This disaster gave rise to the saying "End-to-end is further than you think".)

I would like to say I handled the situation well. I didn't. I panicked. I tried to get the team to agree to cram all the remaining work into the available time. It was Chet Hendrickson who brought me up short with his drawled, "Every other time we've had to estimate a completion date we've estimated the pieces and added them up. What's different about this situation?"

I was worried about my bonus, but I was also worried about my dream of never having to deploy late again. The situation worked out okay. We were certified in March and went live in April.

The system was in production for three years, being decommissioned in 2000. The two issues leading to its termination were technology and funding. By 2000, Java, not Smalltalk, was clearly the dominant object technology. Chrysler didn't want to maintain a system in a little-used language indefinitely. They were already in that situation with another system and it was awkward and expensive. The project had been funded by IT as a pilot in using object technology. IT asked Finance to pay for later phases. Finance refused. The project was cancelled.

The system was reliable, cheap, and easy to maintain and extend. The architecture stayed fluid and appropriate. The defect rate was incredibly low compared with similar projects. The team made it easy to welcome new members and the departure of team members made proportionate impact on the team's effectiveness. The project was a technical success to the end.

The project was also a business success. It proved that object technology was appropriate for large-scale data processing projects. Then the business needs changed. Politically controlled funding pays for software development. Software development funding priorities change rapidly with the shifts in technology and business practices.

This is my story of the beginnings of XP. Since then, much thought and work by many teams have gone into the refinement of the ideas and explorations of the relationship between values, principles, and practices in XP.

Chapter 18

Taylorism and Software

Frederick Taylor was the first industrial engineer. Others before him had studied efficiency in factories, but Taylor came to the field with an intensity and charisma that created the whole field of industrial engineering. Through his work and that of his disciples, most notably Frank and Lillian Gilbreth and Henry Gantt, he brought a rigorous and compelling presentation of the case for systematically improving factory productivity. He picked a powerful metaphor for his teaching, Scientific Management.

When picking descriptive names, it helps to pick a name whose opposite is unappealing. Who could possibly be for "unscientific" management? What Taylor meant by "science" was that to improve factory productivity, he would apply the methods of science: observation, hypothesis, and experimentation. He would observe a worker at a task, devise alternative ways of performing the task, observe these, and pick the best way to do the task. (One of his mottoes was "The One Best Way".) All that was left was to standardize the execution of that task through the whole factory to guarantee improvement.

I don't have space here to describe all the technical, social, and economic impacts of Taylorism, as it came to be called. The bibliography gives you several opportunities for further reading. While Taylorism has some positive effects, it also has some serious shortcomings. These limitations come from three simplifying assumptions:

- ✧ Things usually go according to plan.
- ✧ Micro-optimization leads to macro-optimization.
- ✧ People are mostly interchangeable and need to be told what to do.

Why is Taylorism important for software engineering? No one walks around a development shop with a clipboard and a stopwatch. The problem for software development is that Taylorism implies a social structure of work. While we've lost the rituals and trappings of time-and-motion studies, we have unconsciously inherited this social structure and it is bizarrely unsuited to software development.

The first step of social engineering in Taylorism is the separation of planning from execution. It is the educated engineers who decide how work is to be done and how long it will take. The workers must faithfully execute the assigned task in the assigned way in the allotted time and all will be well. Workers are cogs in a machine. No one wants to think of himself as a cog.

Echoes of Taylor can be heard in software development any time a person in authority makes or changes an estimate for someone else's work. The echoes can also be heard when an "elite" architecture or framework group prescribes precisely how work should be done by someone else.

The second step of Taylorist social engineering is the creation of a separate quality department. Taylor assumed that workers would "soldier" whenever possible (work slowly or badly but not so slowly or badly as to be noticed). He created a separate quality control department to ensure that workers not only worked at the right pace but in the specified way, in order to achieve the right level of quality.

Many software development organizations are directly (and even proudly) Taylorist in having a separate quality organization. Having a separate quality department sends the message that quality is exactly as important to engineering as marketing or sales. No one in engineering is responsible for quality. Someone else is. Putting QA as a separate department within the engineering organization also sends the message that engineering and quality are separate, parallel activities. Separating quality from engineering organizationally makes the job of the quality department punitive instead of constructive.

I am not saying that quality, architecture, or frameworks are unimportant to software development. Quite the contrary. They are too important to be left to Taylorist social structures that impede the flow of communication and feedback vital to creating working, flexible, and inexpensive software in a changing world. We'll see in the next chapter some more recent ideas from the world of manufacturing that provide alternative social structures to meet these goals of productivity and quality.

Chapter 19

Toyota Production System

Toyota is one of the most profitable large auto manufacturers. It makes excellent products, grows fast, has high margins, and makes lots of money. Toyota's goal of going fast is not achieved by straining. Toyota eliminates wasted effort at every step of the process of producing cars. If you eliminate enough waste, soon you go faster than the people who are just trying to go fast.

This chapter focuses on the part of the Toyota Production System (TPS) that actually manufactures cars. Mary and Tom Poppendieck write extensively about the importance of the product development part of TPS to the whole task of delivering value through software.

Their alternative social structure of work is critical to the success of TPS. Every worker is responsible for the whole production line. If anyone spots a defect he pulls a cord that stops the whole line. All the resources of the line are applied to finding the root cause of the problem and fixing it. At first, American workers can't believe this. Chet Hendrickson told me the story of his brother-in-law who worked at a Toyota plant in Kentucky. He saw a defective door go by. His buddy said, "Pull the cord." Nah, he didn't want to get in trouble. Another defective door. Another. Finally, he pulled the cord. He was praised for telling the truth and pointing out flaws. Unlike mass-production lines where someone "down the line" is responsible for quality, in TPS the goal is to make the quality of the line good enough that there is no need for downstream quality assurance. This implies that everyone is responsible for quality.

Individual workers have a lot of say in how work is performed and improved in TPS. Waste is eliminated through kaizen (continuous improvement) events. Workers identify a source of waste, either quality problems or inefficiency. Then, they take the lead in analyzing the problem, performing experiments, and standardizing the results.

TPS eliminates the rigid social stratification found in Taylorist factories. Industrial engineers begin their careers working on the line and always spend a considerable amount of time in the factory. Ordinary workers perform routine maintenance instead of an elite caste of technicians. There is no separate quality organization. The whole organization is a quality organization.

Workers are accountable for the quality of their work because the parts they create are immediately put to use by the next step in the line. This direct coupling of functions was completely counterintuitive to me when I first read about it. I thought that for a mass-production factory to run smoothly there must be a large inventory of parts between any two steps of the process. That way, if the upstream machine stops working, the downstream machine can keep chugging away on the buffer of parts.

TPS turns this thinking on its head. While individual machines may work more smoothly with lots of "work-in-progress" inventory, the factory looked at as a whole doesn't work as well. If you use a part immediately you get the value of the part itself as well as information about whether the upstream machine is working correctly. This view, that parts aren't just parts but also information about their making, leads to pressure to keep all the machines in a line working smoothly and also provides the information necessary to keep the machines working smoothly.

Taiichi Ohno, the spiritual leader of TPS, says the greatest waste is the waste of overproduction. If you make something and can't sell it, the effort that went into making it is lost. If you make something internally in the line and don't use it immediately its information value evaporates. There are also storage costs: you have to haul it to a warehouse; track it while it is there; polish the rust off it when you take it back out again; and risk that you'll never use it at all, in which case you have to pay to haul it away.

Software development is full of the waste of overproduction: fat requirements documents that rapidly grow obsolete; elaborate architectures that are never used; code that goes months without being integrated, tested, and executed in a production environment; and documentation no one reads until it is irrelevant or misleading. While all of these activities are important to software development, we need to use their output immediately in order to get the feedback we need to eliminate waste.

Requirements gathering, for instance, will not improve by having ever more elaborate requirements-gathering processes but by shortening the path between the production of requirements detail and the deployment of the software specified. Using requirements detail immediately implies that requirements gathering isn't a phase that produces a static document; but an activity producing detail, just before it is needed, throughout development.

Many other aspects of TPS also have strong parallels to software development; useful concepts such as cross-training workers, organizing the factory into cells, and writing gain-sharing contracts between customers and suppliers. If you are interested, I recommend that you start with Ohno's *Toyota Production System*.

Chapter 20

Applying XP

Five years ago I thought that if I did a better job of programming, other people would like me and want to follow my example. It turns out that applying XP is not as simplistic as this. XP takes place in a complex social context, so simply applying techniques doesn't give you control of the organization or even your project.

Applying XP and seeing dramatic results takes a while, more like years than weeks. You should see big improvement in the first weeks and months, but those improvements only set the stage for the big leaps forward that happen further down the road. There is so much waste in software development. The waste is rooted more in what we believe and feel than in what we do. Becoming aware of and addressing those beliefs and feelings takes time and experience.

The word "adoption" as applied to a style of software development has all the wrong implications. Taking on a style of software development does not cover or eliminate your pre-existing problems. The problems you have are still your problems. With XP you will have a new context in which to go about solving them. XP is not what addresses them. You are going to address them, in your own way, in your own time, in the context of XP or whatever process you use. While you may have a vision of how you are going to develop in a few years, by the time you get there you'll be developing in your own style. Your own style may be significantly influenced by a vision like XP's, but it'll still be your style.

Starting with XP is more like getting into a pool than adopting a child. There are many ways to get into a pool: you can dip in a toe; you can sit on the edge and dangle your feet; you can walk down the steps; you can perform a smooth, powerful racing dive; or you can do a cannonball, making a lot of noise and getting everyone around you wet. There is not one right way to get in the water.

Once teams start applying XP, there is always the danger of reverting to the old way of doing things. Programmers who know better still change code without writing a failing test first. Managers who know better, who have experienced the benefits of clear and honest communication, still demand more of teams than anyone believes is possible. Organizations that see dramatic improvement elect to revert to old methods and waste in times of stress. Reverting to past behaviors regardless of their effectiveness is common.

Organizational reversion is hard to address because it is out of the team's control. The XP team does a great job, deploys more functionality than originally requested with minimal defects right on time with no extra stress or hours. Another team pulls all-nighters, slashes scope viciously at the last moment, and deploys amid a blizzard of defects. When the organization downsizes, the XP team is fired because the other team showed more "commitment". XP teams work differently, standing out in a way that can have negative social and political effects. Teams need to emphasize their commitment to the organizational goals and show how their style of work supports these goals.

Finding an executive sponsor to champion XP within the organization smooths your interaction with the company while you are transitioning to a new style of work. Expect to be accountable to the person who is standing up for you. If you don't have support from higher up in the organization, your own satisfaction with your team's rapport and productivity may have to suffice.

The way to begin organizational change is still to start with yourself. It is the one change you have control over. First develop your skills, then put them into service. Leading by example is a powerful form of leadership. Dave Thomas and Andy Hunt, the "Pragmatic Programmers", are excellent examples of this strategy.

I was talking recently with a technical lead who told me that he totally supported programmers writing automated tests. "Great," I said, "you've tried JUnit then?"

"Oh, no, I've never written any tests. I just think it's a great idea."

Expecting others to do what you are not willing to try yourself is disrespectful and ineffective. Asking them to take risks you aren't willing to take undermines your relationships and destroys the cohesiveness of the team. This misalignment of authority and responsibility creates distrust. You also lose the opportunity for learning, feedback, and self-improvement.

The strategy of learning skills and putting them into service works at many scales:

- ✧ You learn test-first programming, then share it with your team.
- ✧ Your team learns to estimate and develop story-by-story, then invites internal customers to pick stories.
- ✧ Your organization learns to deploy solid software predictably, then invites external customers to be part of planning.

In each case, the gesture is the same: change myself, then offer the fruits of that change to others. Both steps create value. When I change, it's because I've found a way to improve. When I offer new skills to my customers, I pass along these benefits.

"Continuous" improvement is a bit of a misnomer. It means continuous awareness, responsiveness to feedback, and openness to improvement. When you know how to improve, then you improve. You make a change; observe the effects; then digest the change, turning it into a solid habit. Eventually you hit a plateau from which you can absorb more feedback and identify the next opportunity (Figure 23).

FIGURE 23. "Continuous" learning is not continuous

FIGURE 24. Learning is not a straight line

Sometimes you'll try a new practice only to discover that your performance actually falls (Figure 24).

When this happens, it doesn't mean that improvement is impossible or that the practice you tried is inherently bad. It may mean you don't have enough experience with the practice. It may mean you weren't ready for the new practice, because some hidden prerequisites weren't in place. Change back and address the underlying issues. Later, the practice in question may appear at the top of your improvement list again, and this time you'll be ready.

The course of improvement is not smooth or predictable. It is sensitive to both the context in which it begins and the course of improvement itself. A sequence of practices that worked magic for one team might be a disaster for another.

I don't want to imply that the course of improvement is always slow and tortuous. I have seen teams turn themselves around in weeks. Conditions that facilitate sudden turnarounds are:

- *Aligned values.* The team and organization are willing to accept and work with the XP values.
- *Pain.* The team has been through a recent loss like layoffs or a failed deployment. Clear memory of recent pain makes people more willing to try dramatic changes.

While the course of such improvement looks dramatic and discontinuous, it's really just the normal wavy curve compressed because the team is so receptive to change (Figure 25).

Forcing these conditions for rapid change is not ethical. However, if you find yourself in this situation, you have an opportunity for seemingly miraculous change. It's not magic, just the regular stuff happening very quickly.

FIGURE 25. Rapid learning

Choosing a Coach

The word "coach" implies a balance between being part of the team and having an independent perspective. In the beginning, the coach is the one who spots opportunities for improvement and leads the experiments addressing them. Coaches have experience and perspective and are not enmeshed in the day-to-day group dynamics.

You can apply XP successfully without an experienced coach. Many teams have done it. You won't benefit from the experience and perspective of a coach, but you can learn as you go. Applying XP doesn't happen without leadership though, whether from inside or outside the team.

The values, principles, and practices of XP are best learned by example. You can learn them from someone who has made all the mistakes or you can make the mistakes yourself. I've been on both sides of this learning. People will pair program with me and say, "I thought I knew what test-first programming was, but now I *really* get it. You actually write a *little* test before *every* change." I was also in the position of thinking I understood frequent releases, but when I worked on a team deploying daily I had the same kind of aha experience: "So you *really* deploy new software *every* day." Just because you understand the words doesn't mean you understand. A coach can accelerate your learning.

A coach notices bottlenecks in communication and deals with them. A coach reminds teams to do the simple thing when they are listening to their fears. A coach motivates teams to use the practices; for example, "Have you written a test for that yet?" A coach models effective values and practices. A coach is responsible for the process as a whole, keeping the team working at a sustainable pace and continuing to improve. A coach communicates what he sees in such a way that the team can address problems.

Selecting a coach is an important and challenging decision. A coach should be aligned enough with your existing values to be effective, but firm enough in the XP values to keep leading in that direction. A coach should have enough technical skill to teach what people can't easily learn on their own. Finally, and most importantly, a coach should encourage independence, not dependence. A good coach moves on a little before you think you're ready and leaves behind a team that finds itself firmly on a path to sustainable, profitable, stable, fast, fun software development.

When You Shouldn't Use XP

XP is ineffective in organizations whose actual values are at odds with the XP values. I say "actual values" because many organizations have professed values differing from or contradicting the values revealed by their actions. In XP, you have a set of practices intended to express and reinforce a certain set of values. If an organization's actual values are secrecy, isolation, complexity, timidity, and disrespect; suddenly expressing the opposite values through a new set of practices will cause trouble rather than create improvement.

Chapter 21

Purity

One question that comes up repeatedly is, "Is my team extreme?" People have concocted various charts and metrics to measure "extremeness". When used as a tool for reflection, these make sense. As a scoring mechanism where a score of 10 is twice as good as 5, they are absurd. Expecting a binary or numerical answer to the question, "Is my team extreme?" makes no sense.

I like Tex-Mex food. If I see a restaurant that advertises Tex-Mex food, I kind of know what to expect: spicy food, lots of meat, and beans. If I get served (as my daughter once was in Zurich) a limp tortilla with tomato sauce, Swiss cheese, and a pickle; I'll be disappointed. The question, "Is it Tex-Mex? Is it *really* Tex-Mex?", is important because it sets my expectations for what I'm going to get.

So with the question, "Is my team extreme?" There isn't a binary answer. If someone asks me, "We have a team split between here and Boston, but we're doing everything else on the list of practices. Is that XP?" I can't answer thumbs-up or thumbs-down, nor is my judgement important. Are the team members doing all the things that make sense to them in a sustainable way? That's the question, but only they can answer it.

XP, as a theory, predicts that if you sit together, you'll get better results. Maybe a team is getting good enough results already. Then it is doing fine, really-truly XP or not really-truly XP. If the team wants further improvement, it could increase face-to-face communication by sitting together some or all of the time; intensify the practices already in use; or try practices from areas outside XP—usability, teamwork/communication, human resources, marketing, or sales.

This doesn't mean that any old software development style (or lack thereof) is extreme. The values, principles, and practices are there to provide guidance, challenge, and accountability. "If you aren't working well together, consider trying these things for these reasons to see if you can improve your relationships and your performance." If you just stop writing documentation and use XP as an excuse, you will be called on your behavior by the community. Belligerently saying, "We don't have to write documentation because we're extreme," shows contempt for communication, not an embracing of communication as a value.

There isn't a binary test for whether a person or team is extreme. Lots of teams with different values, principles, and practices successfully create value through software development. It's worse to fail with an XP team than to succeed with a pure waterfall team. The goal is successful and satisfying relationships and projects, not membership in the XP Club.

Saying that your team is extreme sets other people's expectations for your style of communication, your development practices, and the speed and quality of your results.

Certification and Accreditation

Another topic on the same general theme is certification, of either individuals or teams. With a certification process, the certifying agency is staking its reputation on the suitability of certified individuals and accepting some responsibility for the person certified. If board-certified physicians turn out to be incompetent, the board's credibility vanishes.

No certification in computing dares go this far. Who wants to be legally liable for someone else's development choices? If a certifying authority isn't willing to stand behind its certification, it is just printing certificates and collecting money.

There is still a need to know whether a person is legitimately skilled in XP without having to rely solely on his own word. An informal referral network is already in place, but you have to know whom to ask.

The model provided by La Leche League in accrediting the leaders who hold informational meetings for nursing mothers is appealing. In this model both parties retain full responsibility for their behavior.

Accreditation acknowledges to the public that we both agree that you are what you say you are. It says that the individual leader's values are aligned with the organization's for the purpose of supporting other mothers.

LLL leader applicants begin by being invited by an existing leader. The inviting leader and a volunteer accrediter join to mentor the applicant and evaluate her knowledge and skill. The process includes:

⬥ Evaluating the applicant's knowledge of the technical, social, and organizational skills needed to lead meetings.
⬥ Leading meetings with the applicant and critiquing her performance.
⬥ Reviewing a paper written by the applicant reflecting on her experience of nursing and mothering.
⬥ Social interaction with other leaders.
⬥ Being publicly introduced to the group at a regional conference.
⬥ Encouragement and support.

This model is a much more fruitful direction for certification than the models currently practiced in computing. The meaning of certification is necessarily subjective, whatever its trappings of formality and rigor. In the end, you're an XPer when you hold XP's values and incorporate XP principles in your daily practice. XPers will recognize each other in the community. Formalizing this process would give XP a clearer presence, help align employer/employee expectations, and give us a way to mentor and support each other as leaders as we go about our business of changing the way the world thinks of software development.

Chapter 22

Offshore Development

Offshore development provides a case study for applying XP's values, principles, and practices outside their "sweet spot," the small team sitting together.

I don't like the political and racial overtones of the word "offshore": high-paid white people taking advantage of low-paid dark people and then complaining about "them" taking "our" jobs. "Offshore" implies an imbalance of power, the kind of imbalance that can easily derail software development. I use the term "multi-site" here because XP applies similarly to all geographically dispersed teams.

There are lots of reasons to run a project at multiple sites. Salary differential is only one of these reasons. The database people may be in Toronto and the telecom people in Denver. No matter the reason for considering multi-site development, it always comes down to a business decision: weighing whether the waste created by not sitting together is more than offset by other advantages.

The values of XP are just as suited to multi-site development as they are to teams that sit together. Embrace feedback more tightly because of the natural isolation created by distance. Nurture communication more because of the unavailability of face-to-face, full-spectrum interaction. You'll have to work harder to achieve simplicity because you won't have as many chances for serendipitous discovery of excess complexity. Courage is just as important as it is in any other setting. Respecting everyone on a distributed team is even more important because of differences in culture and lifestyle.

Some of the practices will have to be modified for multi-site projects. For example, planning may have to occur more frequently than weekly to maintain a sense of conversation and to avoid situations in which one site dictates what another site must do. Beware of abandoning practices just because they seem difficult. The single code base is more important as a point of connection in multi-site development than when sitting together. Work to overcome whatever technical obstacles arise to keep the team working together on the same program.

When it comes to principles, the principle of mutual benefit is the one that bears most on the whole question of multi-site development, especially when talking about jobs being shifted to other sites. The most beneficial outcome for everyone involved is well-paying jobs (relatively speaking) for programmers everywhere and delighted customers who are willing to pay for much more software because it is so much more valuable. Jobs aren't going in search of low salaries. Jobs are going in search of integrity and accountability. If integrity and accountability can better be supplied by a separate company many time zones away, customers will pay the necessary price in difficult communication to get them. If the software industry learns to create more value at lower cost, the increase in demand will more than make up for the temporary loss of jobs in any one location.

In high-cost-base areas, improved efficiency, integrity, and accountability are imperative for survival. The days of one hundred expensive contractors without accountability working on one project are numbered. The same project will be done with ten efficient and accountable programmers or it will go elsewhere. To maintain technical employment in high-cost areas, dramatic improvement is necessary. High-cost-base teams need to focus on high-leverage projects, where the strength of direct communication is most valuable, improving their efficiency so overall costs are on par with doing a similar project elsewhere.

To compete, low-cost-base teams need to increase the value they create too. The technical and marketing advantages of Taylorist improvement programs like the Capability Maturity Model have nearly run their course. Just because you can afford to throw lots of bodies at a problem doesn't mean that is the most profitable way to solve it. Organizations addicted to high labor counts need to gradually reduce their team sizes while increasing throughput.

Here are two scenarios for the future of global software development. In the first, high-cost-base countries try to stop the clock, using politics to allow them to program as usual. Low-cost-base countries have no incentive to improve. Software development stagnates.

In the second scenario, programmers worldwide strive to eliminate software development waste in all its many forms. Businesses find many new uses for a new generation of reliable, effective, and cheap software. The global market for software booms. All countries employ more programmers than a decade before.

Improvement is not a foregone conclusion. Software development could stay on its current path of creeping increments. Without dramatic improvement, though, the global market for software will stagnate as more attractive investments are found in manufacturing and biotechnology. To encourage software development as a craft and a business through the next fifty years, I hope that programmers everywhere will accept the challenge of producing much more valuable software. I believe the expanding market will more than make up for losses in any one location because of increased efficiency and multi-site development.

Chapter 23

The Timeless Way
of Programming

The architect Christopher Alexander describes a time not so long ago
when people knew how to design and build spaces for themselves,
uniquely fitted to their own needs and to their climate and culture.
Growing up I heard stories of my carpenter great-grandfather. Whenever his family moved to a new town, he would immediately begin
doing odd jobs and saving money. When he had enough, he would buy
lumber and build a house. My great-grandfather wasn't trained as an
architect, but he knew how to design a house that would suit his family.

Alexander notes that an architect's selfish interests are not aligned
with the client's. The architect wants to get the job done quickly and
win awards, but is missing critical information: how the client wants to
live. Alexander's dream was to return the power of designing space to
the people whose lives were most affected by it.

Alexander collected architectural patterns as a means to this end,
encoding good solutions to the problems known to recur in designing
and building homes. The patterns were never intended as an end in
themselves, but as a means of balancing power between professional
designers and those who live and work in the space being designed.

Alexander's vision still included a role for architects. Every project
has unique problems as well as tediously predictable ones. The key to
designing space that is alive is joining the deep understanding of individual preferences and social relationships held by the users of the space
with the deep technical understanding of the architect. Bringing these
two perspectives together in harmony, with neither dominating the

other, enables the design and construction of a space that meets human needs and keeps the rain out too.

As I began to work in software development, I found the same imbalance of power that Alexander fought in architecture. I grew up in Silicon Valley, where engineering was king. "We'll give you what you need even if you don't know you need it," was the often-explicit motto. Software written this way tends to be long on technical virtuosity and short on utility.

With more experience I began to see the opposite imbalance, where business concerns dominated development. Deadlines and scope set only for business reasons do not maintain the integrity of the team. The concerns of users and sponsors are important, but the needs of the developers are also valid. All three need to inform each other.

My bias in writing XP originally was towards the programmers. That's my background. That's who I identified with on teams. However, the past five years have taught me that software development can't be "the programmers and a bunch of other people" if the goal is excellence. Without balance between the concerns of everyone involved, some people will be unable to contribute to development, and their views are important to the team's success. My goal is now to help teams routinely bring technical and business concerns into harmony.

Harmony and balance are the aims of XP. Writing tests is a good thing in itself, but it is only preparation for the bigger task: fostering strong relationships between the diverse people who come together to make money with software. Without a change of heart, all the practices and principles in the world will produce only small, short-term gains. You and the rest of your team share a fate. Act like it and you may come to believe it.

Alexander ultimately failed in his attempt to balance power between the designers and users of space. The architects didn't want to give up any of their power and the clients didn't know to demand any. Programs are not buildings and software development is not construction. Our materials are not their materials and our social structures are not locked into millennia of fixed relationships. We, in software, have the opportunity to create new social structures in which technical excellence is joined with business vision to create new products and services of unique value. This is our advantage.

XP relies on the growth of powerful programmers; able to quickly estimate, implement, and deploy reliable software. These programmers turn over business decision making to the business-oriented part of the team. The appropriate sharing of power and responsibility among the team may seem utopian. This balance is contingent on mutual respect. There is no absolute power. The power of XP evaporates if misused. Each manipulated estimate, each job rushed through without pride, puts the team that much further from its potential power. XP relies on each member of the team; including executives, managers, and customers; to be fully committed and contribute what he can. A team working together can accomplish more than the sum of its members' separate efforts. Sharing power is pragmatic, not idealistic.

Realizing the potential in software requires teamwork. The first fifty years of computing have gone pretty well. I've heard lectures predicting that the next century is the century of biology, not computing. Computing will be relegated to a supporting role. I believe this will be true if software continues business as usual. If our software tools and techniques creep forward, biology will soon overtake software as a driver of social and economic change.

Tools and techniques change often, but they don't change a lot. People, however, change slowly but deeply. The challenge of XP is to encourage deep change, to renew individual values and mutual relationships to give software a seat at the table for the next fifty years. Unleashing the potential of the human spirit will lead to a future for computing that we can't yet imagine.

Chapter 24

Community and XP

A supportive community is a great asset in software development. This is true whether the community in question is the team itself, like-minded software developers in the local area, or the global community. Communities provide a safe place to voice problems and share experiences. Communities are a good place to find a sympathetic ear and give the gift of listening.

Community is important because everyone needs support sometimes. Relationships provide a safe, stable place to experiment. You can check out your new experiences with others to find out to what degree your discomfort is a normal reaction to change. In turn, when someone else in the community needs perspective, you can listen and, if asked, offer your opinion.

Listening is a far more important skill inside a community than talking. For open, honest communication to take place in a community, the participants must feel safe and understood. Sometimes all a speaker wants is to be heard. Kvetching, dumping, venting, showing off your cleverness, whatever you call it—if the response is a torrent of unasked-for advice, the community is not safe. If the speaker has something to say from his heart, he needs to be confident that it is safe to speak and that he'll be acknowledged.

Communities can also be a place to study together. XP includes many skills that improve with practice. There are local area XP groups that study topics of interest to the participants. If there isn't such a group in your area, consider starting one. Groups inside companies can be useful. However, having diverse perspectives reflecting your experience is valuable, especially if they aren't bought into the same corporate culture you work with every day.

Communities also provide accountability, a place to be held to your word. Today you may provide that service for your fellows, tomorrow they for you. Accountability is particularly important when making changes. Trying shortcuts or reverting in other ways might appear attractive in the moment. They are harder to justify if you know you will have to report you behavior to your peers. Accountability underscores the need for communities to be safe. Respecting confidentiality, offering advice only when asked, and suspending judgement all contribute to safety.

Communities are a place for questioning and doubt. Each individual's opinion holds value to the community. Conflict and disagreement are the seeds of learning together. Squelching conflict is a sign of weakness in a community. Valuable ideas can withstand scrutiny. Members of a community don't commit to full-time unanimity; they agree to respect each other while they work out their disagreements. Compliance is not a requirement for participation in a safe community.

XP has several active communities online that you can easily join. The most active is hosted by Yahoo!, and can be found at *http://groups.yahoo.com/group/extremeprogramming*. Different languages also have their own XP mailing lists, which you can find by searching online. You can also find local users' groups online. Most meet once a month, but some meet as frequently as once a week.

Participate in communities, local and global. Look for communities that encourage you to be your best self. If you can't find such a community, start one yourself. If you are wrestling with difficult questions, you are not alone. As a community we can accomplish more than we ever could in isolation.

Chapter 25

Conclusion

I codified XP to make life better for programmers. Along the way, XP became a way of being in the world for me. However, it is a way that requires me to think about my own values and align my behavior with them. What I discovered is that there is no improvement without first improving myself.

The key to XP is integrity, acting in harmony with my true values. As soon as I set integrity as my goal, I discovered that the values I actually held were not the ones I wanted the world to think I held. The past five years have been a journey of changing my actual values into those I wanted to hold.

I have been far from perfect on this journey. Some days I'm keenly aware of how far short I fall from my own ideals. There are times, though, when it all comes together, when my values match my ideals and my behavior flows naturally from them. It is then that I know the trip is worth continuing.

With XP, I work to become worthy of respect and offer respect to others. I'm content to do my best and strive always to improve. I hold values I am proud of and act in harmony with those values.

XP values are worth putting into practice in the business world. Besides having a life you can live in comfort, you develop a style of work based on respectful relationships that are good for all involved. You produce software that actively and positively contributes to the world. You work creatively and energetically.

I have seen people applying XP bring renewed hope to their software development and their lives. You know enough to get started. I encourage you to start now. Think about your values. Make conscious choices to live in harmony with them. Pick a practice to begin along your path. If you are looking for a world in which you can be comfortable, live in balance and do good business; XP is a way of thinking about and acting on your ideals.

Annotated Bibliography

Reading a wide range of books around a topic adds to the richness of my understanding. Here are a few suggestions for interesting reading on ideas related to XP.

Philosophy

Sue Bender, *Plain and Simple: A Woman's Journey to the Amish*, Harper-Collins, 1989; ISBN 0062501860.

> Examines the value of simplicity and clarity.

Leonard Coren, *Wabi-Sabi: For Artists, Designers, Poets, and Philosophers*, Stone Bridge Press, 1994; ISBN 1880656124.

> Wabi-sabi is an aesthetic celebration of the rough and functional.

Richard Coyne, *Designing Information Technology in the Postmodern Age: From Method to Metaphor*, MIT Press, 1995; ISBN 0262032287.

> Discusses the differences between modernist and postmodernist thought including an excellent discussion of the importance of metaphors.

Philip B. Crosby, *Quality Is Free: The Art of Making Quality Certain*, Mentor Books, 1992; ISBN 0451625854.

> Breaks out of the zero-sum model of the four variables—time, scope, cost, and quality. You can't get software out the door faster

by lowering quality. Instead, you get software out the door faster by raising quality.

George Lakoff and Mark Johnson, *Philosophy in the Flesh: The Embodied Mind and Its Challenge to Western Thought*, Basic Books, 1998; ISBN 0465056733.

More good discussion of metaphors and thinking. Also, the description of how metaphors blend together. The old software metaphors drawn from civil engineering, mathematics, and so on are slowly morphing into uniquely software engineering metaphors.

Bill Mollison and Rena Mia Slay, *Introduction to Permaculture*, Ten Speed Press, 1997; ISBN 0908228082.

High-intensity use in the Western world has generally been associated with exploitation and exhaustion. Permaculture is a thoughtful discipline of farming that aims for sustainable high-intensity use of the land through the synergistic effects of simple practices. This has some parallelism to XP. For example, most growth occurs at the interactions between elements. Permaculture maximizes interactions with spirals of interplantings and lakes with wildly irregular edges. XP maximizes interactions with on-site customers and pair programming.

Attitude

Christopher Alexander, *Notes on the Synthesis of Form*, Harvard University Press, 1970; ISBN 0674627512.

Alexander started by thinking about design as decisions resolving conflicting constraints, leading to further decisions to resolve the remaining constraints.

Christopher Alexander, *The Timeless Way of Building*, Oxford University Press, 1979; ISBN 0195024028.

Outlines Christopher Alexander's view of architecture and construction. The relationship described between designers/builders and the users of buildings is much the same as the relationship between the programmers and the customer.

Ross King, *Brunelleschi's Dome: How a Renaissance Genius Reinvented Architecture*, Penguin Books, 2001; ISBN 0142000159.

> Extreme architecture and construction. Brunelleschi refused to be intimidated by problems, a great example of the principle of opportunity.

Field Marshal Irwin Rommel, *Attacks: Rommel*, Athena, 1979; ISBN 0960273603.

> Examples of proceeding in apparently hopeless circumstances.

Dave Thomas and Andy Hunt, *The Pragmatic Programmer*, Addison-Wesley, 1999; ISBN 020161622X.

> Dave and Andy couple technical skill with an attitude that I call extreme.

Frank Thomas and Ollie Johnston, *Disney Animation: The Illusion of Life*, Hyperion, 1995; ISBN 0786860707.

> Describes how the team structure at Disney evolved over the years to deal with changing business and technology. There are also lots of good tips for user interface designers and some really cool pictures.

Office Space, Mike Judge, director, 1999; ASIN B000069HPL.

> A view of life in a cubicle.

The Princess Bride, Rob Reiner, director, MGM/UA Studios, 1987; ASIN B00005LOKQ.

> "We'll never make it out alive."
> "Nonsense. You're just saying that because no one ever has."

Emergent Processes

Christopher Alexander, Sara Ishikawa, and Murray Silverstein, *A Pattern Language*, Oxford University Press, 1977; ISBN 0195019199.

> An example of a system of rules intended to produce emergent properties. We can argue about whether the rules are successful or

not, but the rules themselves make interesting reading. Also, an excellent if too-brief discussion of the design of workspaces.

James Gleick, *Chaos: Making a New Science*, Penguin USA, 1988; ISBN 0140092501.

A gentle introduction to chaos theory.

Stuart Kauffman, *At Home in the Universe: The Search for Laws of Self-Organization and Complexity*, Oxford University Press, 1996; ISBN 0195111303.

A slightly less gentle introduction to chaos theory.

Roger Lewin, *Complexity: Life at the Edge of Chaos*, Collier Books, 1994; ISBN 0020147953.

More chaos theory.

Margaret Wheatley, *Leadership and the New Science*, Berrett-Koehler Pub, 1994; ISBN 1881052443.

Uses self-organizing systems as a metaphor for management.

Systems

Albert-Laszlo Barabasi, *Linked: How Everything Is Connected to Everything Else and What It Means*, Plume Books, 2003; ISBN 0452284392.

Many of the networks in programming, social and technical, are "scale-free" as described in this book.

Eliyahu Goldratt and Jeff Cox, *The Goal: A Process of Ongoing Improvement*, North River Press, 1992; ISBN 0884270610.

The Theory of Constraints is a way of understanding systems and improving their throughput.

Gerald Weinberg, *Quality Software Management: Volume 1, Systems Thinking*, Dorset House, 1991; ISBN 0932633226.

A system and notation for thinking about systems of interacting elements.

Norbert Weiner, *Cybernetics*, MIT Press, 1961; ISBN 1114239089.

A deeper, more difficult introduction to systems.

Warren Witherell and Doug Evrard, *The Athletic Skier*, Johnson Books, 1993; ISBN 1555661173.

A system of interrelated rules for skiing. The big improvements come when adopting the last few rules because being a little off balance is very different than being on balance.

People

Tom DeMarco and Timothy Lister, *Peopleware*, Dorset House, 1999; ISBN 0932633439.

Following *The Psychology of Computer Programming*, this book expanded the practical dialog about programs as written by people, and in particular as written by teams of people. This book was my source for the principle of "accepted responsibility."

Tom DeMarco, *Slack: Getting Past Burnout, Busywork, and the Myth of Total Efficiency*, Broadway, 2002; ISBN 0767907698.

Applying the concept of margins to software development.

Carlo d'Este, *Fatal Decision: Anzio and the Battle for Rome*, Harper-Collins, 1991; ISBN 006092148X.

An example of ego getting in the way of clear thinking.

Robert Kanigel, *The One Best Way: Frederick Winslow Taylor and the Enigma of Efficiency*, Penguin, 1999; ISBN 0140260803.

A biography of Taylor that puts his work into a context that helps show the limits of his thinking.

Gary Klein, *Sources of Power*, MIT Press, 1999; ISBN 0262611465.

A simple, readable text on how experienced people make decisions in difficult situations.

Alfie Kohn, *Punished By Rewards: The Trouble with Gold Stars, Incentive Plans, A's, Praise, and Other Bribes*, Mariner Books, 1999; ISBN 0618001816.

This book shook my illusion that I could control other people by giving them just the right kind of reward.

Thomas Kuhn, *The Structure of Scientific Revolutions*, University of Chicago Press, 1996; ISBN 0226458083.

How paradigms become the dominant paradigm. Paradigm shifts have predictable effects.

Patrick Lencioni, *The Five Dysfunctions of a Team: A Leadership Fable*, Jossey-Bass, 2002; ISBN 0787960756.

An easy-to-read description of some of the things that can go wrong on teams and what you can do about it.

Scott McCloud, *Understanding Comics*, Harper Perennial, 1994; ISBN 006097625X.

The last couple of chapters talk about why people write comics. This made me think about why I write programs. There is also good material about the connection between the craft of comics and the art of comics, with parallels to the craft of writing programs (testing, refactoring) and the art of writing programs. There is also good material for user-interface designers about communicating with the spaces between things, and packing information into small spaces without clutter.

Geoffrey A. Moore, *Crossing the Chasm: Marketing and Selling High-Tech Products to Mainstream Customers*, HarperBusiness, 1999; ISBN 0066620023.

Paradigm shifts from a business perspective. Some of the barriers to the acceptance of new ideas are predictable and have simple strategies to address them.

Marshall Rosenberg and Lucy Leu, *Nonviolent Communication: A Language of Life: Create Your Life, Your Relationships, and Your World in Harmony with Your Values*, PuddleDancer Press, 2003; ISBN 1892005034.

Nonviolent communication aims to help people separate observation from judgement, hear the deeper needs expressed and state their own needs clearly.

Frederick Winslow Taylor, *The Principles of Scientific Management*, 2nd ed., Institute of Industrial Engineers, 1998 (1st ed. 1911); ISBN 0898061822.

This is the book that spawned "Taylorism." Specialization and strict divide-and-conquer served to produce more cars cheaper. These principles make no sense as strategies for software development: no business sense and no human sense.

Barbara Tuchman, *Practicing History*, Ballantine Books, 1991; ISBN 0345303636.

A thoughtful historian thinks about how she does history. Like *Understanding Comics*, this book is good for reflecting on why you do what you do.

Colin M. Turnbull, *The Forest People: A Study of the Pygmies of the Congo*, Simon & Schuster, 1961; ISBN 0671640992.

A society with plentiful resources has a mentality of sufficiency, which leads to mutually beneficial relationships and abundant living.

———, *The Mountain People*, Simon & Schuster, 1972; ISBN 0671640984.

A society with scarce resources. A model of scarcity leads to horrific consequences.

Mary Walton and W. Edwards Deming, *The Deming Management Method*, Perigee, 1988; ISBN 0399550011.

Deming explicitly addresses fear as a barrier to performance. Most readings of Deming focus on statistical quality-control methods, but there is much here about the effects of human emotion.

Gerald Weinberg, *Quality Software Management: Volume 3, Congruent Action*, Dorset House, 1994; ISBN 0932633285.

> When you say one thing and do another, bad things happen. This book talks about how to be congruent yourself, how to recognize incongruencies in others, and what to do about it.

———, *The Psychology of Computer Programming*, Dorset House, 1998; ISBN 0932633420.

> First to recognize that programs are written by and for people.

———, *The Secrets of Consulting*, Dorset House, 1986; ISBN 0932633013.

> Strategies for introducing change.

Project Management

David Anderson, *Agile Management for Software Engineering: Applying the Theory of Constraints for Business Results*, Prentice Hall 2004; ISBN 0131424602.

> Application of the Theory of Constraints to software development. Each iteration removes a limitation of the system. Work that doesn't remove a limitation is waste.

Kent Beck and Martin Fowler, *Planning Extreme Programming*, Addison-Wesley, 2000; ISBN 0201710919.

> Technical details about the planning process in XP. Real time estimates give more accurate information and a higher level of accountability than the point system.

Fred Brooks, *The Mythical Man-Month, Anniversary Edition*, Addison-Wesley, 1995; ISBN 0201835959.

> Stories to get you thinking about the four variables. The anniversary edition also has an interesting dialog around the famous "No Silver Bullet" article.

Mike Cohn, *User Stories Applied: For Agile Software Development*, Addison-Wesley, 2004; ISBN 0321205685.

How to plan and track projects feature by feature.

Brad Cox and Andy Novobilski, *Object-Oriented Programming—An Evolutionary Approach*, *Second Edition*, Addison-Wesley, 1991; ISBN 0201548348.

Expounds an electrical engineering paradigm of software development.

Ward Cunningham, "Episodes: A Pattern Language of Competitive Development," in *Pattern Languages of Program Design 2*, John Vlissides, ed., Addison-Wesley, 1996; ISBN 0201895277 (also *http://c2.com/ppr/episodes.html*).

A discussion of short-cycle programming.

Tom DeMarco, *Controlling Software Projects*, Yourdon Press, 1982; ISBN 0131717111.

Examples of creating and using feedback to measure software projects.

Tom DeMarco and Tim Lister, *Waltzing with Bears: Managing Risk on Software Projects*, Dorset House, 2003; ISBN 0932633609.

XP provides many opportunities for risk management, but you still have to manage the risk. This book contains many ideas for taking risks with your eyes open.

Tom Gilb, *Principles of Software Engineering Management*, Addison-Wesley, 1988; ISBN 0201192462.

A strong case for evolutionary delivery—small releases, constant refactoring, intense dialog with the customer.

Ivar Jacobson, Magnus Christerson, Parik Jonsson, and Gunnar Overgaard, *Object-Oriented Software Engineering: A Case Driven Approach*, Addison-Wesley, 1992; ISBN 0201544350.

My source for driving development from stories (use cases).

Ivar Jacobson, Grady Booch, and James Rumbaugh, *The Unified Software Development Process*, Addison-Wesley, 1999; ISBN 0201571692.

UP contains short iterations, an emphasis on metaphor, and uses stories to drive development. UP is usually document-driven and has less rigorous testing procedures.

Philip Metzger, *Managing a Programming Project*, Prentice Hall, 1973; ISBN 0135507561.

The earliest programming project management text I've been able to find. There are nuggets here, but the perspective is pure Taylorism. Out of 200 pages, he spends only two paragraphs on maintenance.

Charles Poole and Jan Willem Huisman, "Using Extreme Programming in a Maintenance Environment," in *IEEE Software*, November/December 2001, pp. 42–50.

One team's results of applying XP to product maintenance: 60% reduction in cost and 66% reduction in the time to fix defects.

Mary Poppendieck and Tom Poppendieck, *Lean Software Development*, Addison-Wesley, 2003; ISBN 0321150783.

Applies the ideas of lean production and lean product development to software.

Jennifer Stapleton, *DSDM, Dynamic Systems Development Method: The Method in Practice*, Addison-Wesley, 1997; ISBN 0201178893.

DSDM is one perspective on bringing rapid application development under control without giving up its benefits.

Hirotaka Takeuchi and Ikujiro Nonaka, "The new product development game," *Harvard Business Review* [1986], 86116:137–146.

A consensus-oriented approach to evolutionary delivery with implications for scaling projects.

Jane Wood and Denise Silver, *Joint Application Development*, 2nd edition, John Wiley and Sons, 1995; ISBN 0471042994.

JAD facilitators facilitate without directing, give power to people who know best how to make a decision, and eventually fade away. JAD is focused on creating a requirements document that the developers and customers agree can and should be implemented.

Programming

David Astels, *Test Driven Development: A Practical Guide*, Prentice Hall, 2003; ISBN 0131016490.

A tutorial on test-driven development.

Kent Beck, *JUnit Pocket Guide*, O'Reilly, 2004; ISBN 0596007434.

The JUnit testing framework and how to use it.

——, *Smalltalk Best Practice Patterns*, Prentice Hall, 1996; ISBN 013476904X.

Patterns for small-scale design and communicating through your code.

——, *Test-Driven Development: By Example*, Addison-Wesley, 2002; ISBN 0321146530.

An introduction to test-first programming and incremental design. The best feature is the list of TDD patterns.

Kent Beck and Erich Gamma, "Test Infected: Programmers Love Writing Tests," in *Java Report,* July 1998, volume 3, number 7, pp. 37–50.

Writing automated tests with JUnit, the Java version of the xUnit testing framework.

Jon Bentley, *Writing Efficient Programs*, Prentice Hall, 1982; ISBN 0139702512.

Cures for the "it ain't gonna be fast enough" blues.

Edward Dijkstra, *A Discipline of Programming*, Prentice Hall, 1976; ISBN 013215871X.

Programming-as-mathematics. Dijkstra searches for beauty through programming.

Eric Evans, *Domain-Driven Design: Tackling Complexity in the Heart of Software*, Addison-Wesley, 2003; ISBN 0321125215.

Lays out a pragmatic road map to clearer communication between business and technical people.

Brian Foote and Joe Yoder, "Big Ball of Mud," *Pattern Languages of Program Design 4*, edited by Neil Harrison, Brian Foote, and Hans Rohnert, Addison-Wesley, 2000; ISBN 0201433044.

What happens when you don't invest enough in incremental design.

Martin Fowler, *Analysis Patterns*, Addison-Wesley, 1996; ISBN 0201895420.

A common vocabulary for making analysis decisions. Analysis patterns help you understand business structures that impact software development.

Martin Fowler, ed., *Refactoring: Improving the Design of Existing Code*, Addison-Wesley, 1999; ISBN 0201485672.

A definitive reference for refactoring.

Martin Fowler and Pramod Sadalage, "Evolutionary Database Design," January 2003, *http://www.martinfowler.com/articles/evodb.html*.

A simple strategy for incrementally designing databases.

Erich Gamma, Richard Helms, Ralph Johnson, and John M. Vlissides, *Design Patterns: Elements of Reusable Object-Oriented Software*, Addison-Wesley, 1995; ISBN 0201633612.

A common vocabulary for making design decisions.

Joshua Kerievsky, *Refactoring to Patterns*, Addison-Wesley, 2004; ISBN 0321213351.

Bridges the gap between design patterns and refactoring. Useful for learning how to design incrementally.

Donald E. Knuth, *Literate Programming*, Stanford University, 1992; ISBN 0937073814.

A communication-oriented programming method. Literate programs, while difficult to maintain, remind us how much there is to communicate.

Steve McConnell, *Code Complete: A Practical Handbook of Software Construction, Second Edition*, Microsoft Press, 2004; ISBN 0735619670.

What you need to know to be a professional developer. Weighs how much care you can profitably put into coding.

Bertrand Meyer, *Object-Oriented Software Construction*, Prentice Hall, 1997; ISBN 0136291554.

Design by contract is an alternative or extension to unit testing.

David Saff and Michael D. Ernst, "An Experimental Evaluation of Continuous Testing During Development," in *ISSTA 2004, Proceedings of the 2004 International Symposium on Software Testing and Analysis* (Boston, MA, USA), July 12-14, 2004, pp. 76-85.

Continuous testing provides more continuous feedback while programming.

Other

Barry Boehm, *Software Engineering Economics*, Prentice Hall, 1981; ISBN 0138221227.

The standard reference for thinking about how much software costs and why.

Stewart Brand, *How Buildings Learn: What Happens After They Are Built*, Penguin Books, 1995; ISBN 0140139966.

Even supposedly rigid structures undergo growth and change.

Malcolm Gladwell, *The Tipping Point: How Little Things Can Make a Big Difference*, Back Bay Books, 2002; ISBN 0316346624.

How ideas catch on.

Larry Gonick and Mark Wheelis, *The Cartoon Guide to Genetics*, Harper-Perennial Library, 1991; ISBN 0062730991.

A demonstration of the power of drawings as a communication medium.

John Hull, *Options, Futures, and Other Derivatives*, Prentice Hall, 1997; ISBN 0132643677.

The standard reference on options pricing.

Nancy Margulies with Nusa Mall, *Mapping Inner Space: Second Edition*, Zephyr Press, 2002; ISBN 1569761388.

Ways to express your thoughts graphically. Enhances communication between linear and non-linear thinkers.

Taiichi Ohno, *Toyota Production System: Beyond Large-Scale Production*, Productivity Press, 1988; ISBN 0915299143.

Provides an interesting contrast with *Principles of Scientific Management*. Ohno's stirring manifesto of business accomplishment achieved with a philosophy of respect for all participants.

Edward Tufte, *The Visual Display of Quantitative Information*, Graphics Press, 1992; ISBN 096139210X.

More techniques for communicating numerical information through pictures. Good for understanding how best to present graphs of metrics, for example. Plus, the book is beautifully published.

Index

A

Abundant living, 167
Accepted responsibility, 4, 165
Accomplishment, as human need, 24
Accountability
    community and, 158
    executive role and, 78
Accounting, for expense vs. investment, 113
Accreditation, XP, 146–147
Action, reflection following, 30
Adopting XP. *See* XP, applying
Alexander, Christopher, 153–154
Analysis, decision making, 172
Andres-Beck, Beth, 104
Anxiety, accompanying change, 57
Application development. *See* Software development
Architects, team roles, 75–76
Architecture
    design and, 154–155
    fluidity, 128
    tests and, 75–76
Architecture, of buildings, 162, 163
Artifacts, of development, 66–67
Attitude, bibliographic references, 162–163

Auditing, projects prior to release, 116
Authority
    misalignment of authority and responsibility, 141
Automated builds, 49
Automated tests, 100–101, 171
awareness, of need for change, 56–57

B

Baby steps, 33, 53
Belonging
    human needs, 24
    team approach and, 39
Beta testing, 101
Bibliography, 161–174
    attitudes, 162–163
    emergent processes, 163–164
    people, 165–168
    philosophy, 161–162
    programming, 171–174
    project management, 168–171
    systems, 164–165
Big bang integration, 30, 87
Big deployments, 63
Biology, in 21st Century, 155

Boehm, Barry, 52
Bottlenecks
    coach noticing, 143
    identifying, 47, 86–87
    Theory of Constraints and, 85–86
Brand, Stewart, 104, 174
Breaks, in work day, 41–42
Budgets, 94–95
Business
    business interests dominating
        development, 154
    business interests sharing responsi-
        bility with programmers, 155
    paradigm shifts and, 166
    relationships, 1

C

Capability Maturity Model, 150
Capital expenditures, 113
Certification, XP, 146–147
Change
    accountability and, 158
    adapting to, 11
    awareness of need for, 56–57
    baby steps and, 33
    changing one thing at a time, 55
    costs of, 52
    deciding what to change first, 56
    factors in rapid change, 142
    feedback and, 19
    opportunities for, 30–31
    people and, 155
    speed of, 56
    starting with yourself, 57
    strategies for, 168
Chaos theory, 164
Charts, in Informative Workspace,
    41
Chrysler Smalltalk project, 125–129
    estimation, 127–128
    incremental design, 127

success of, 128–129
    team creation, 126–127
    trouble indicators, 126
Clarity, bibliographic reference, 161
Coach, selecting, 143–144
Code
    code and tests, 66–67, 101–102
    communicating through, 171
    defect levels and, 98
    eliminating duplication of, 108
    future users, 26
    as key in software development, xix
    profitability of, 173
    sharing responsibility for, 66
    single code base vs. multiple code
        streams, 67–68
    team approach to, 17
    test-first programming and, 50
    traceability of changes to, 116–117
    trust and, 51
    waste and, 137
Code Complete (McConnell), 104
Coe, Bob, 126
Cohesion, of code, 50
Collective ownership, 66. *See also*
    Responsibility
Comics, 166
Commitment, waste created by over-
    commitment, 48
Communication
    between business and technical
        people, 172
    courage and, 21
    credibility and, 48
    documentation and, 146
    drawings as, 174
    embracing as a value, 146
    feedback and, 20
    listening skills vs. talking skills, 157
    multi-site development and, 149
    nonviolent, 167

product managers encouraging, 78
programming as form of, 173
project managers responsibility for, 76–77
simplicity and, 19
as value guiding development, 18
Community, XP, 157–160
Computing, in 21st Century, 155
Conflict
community and, 158
diversity and, 29
Conquer-and-divide, 112
Consensus, in project management, 170
Constraints. *See* Theory of Constraints
Continuous improvement, 141–142
Continuous integration
collective ownership and, 66
as primary practice, 49–50
Contracts, ongoing negotiation of scope, 69
Contributing to Eclipse (Gamma), 51
Control
fallacy of working longer to regain, 41
illusion of being able to control others, xxii
of people, 166
quality and, 32, 169
scope as basis of, 33
Cooperation, 18, 93
Costs
changes, 52
code development, 173
defects, 97
finding defects early and, 99
options pricing, 174
project management and, 92
redundancy, 31

software development, 173
variable in zero-sum model, 161–162
Coupling, of code, 50–51
Courage
balancing with other values, 21
executive role and, 78
multi-site development and, 149
as value guiding development, 20–21
Credibility, 48
Customers
development artifacts of value to, 66–67
driving system content, 12
evolutionary delivery and, 169
features controlled by, 128
interaction designers working with, 75
involvement of, xvi, 61–62
technical writers and, 80
Whole Team practice and, 39

D
Daily deployment, xvi, 68–69, 143
Daily focus, of incremental design, 103
Database design strategy, 107–108, 172
DCI (Defect Cost Increase), 98–99
Deadlines, business concerns dominating, 154
Decision making
analysis decisions, 172
design decision, 172
in difficult situations, 165
Defect Cost Increase (DCI), 98–99
Defects, 119–121
acceptable levels of, 97–98
defect rate in Smalltalk project, 128
incremental design and, 52

Defects, *continued*
  metrics for defects after
    deployment, 79
  redundancy and, 31
  root cause analysis, 64–65
  tests for reducing rate of, 5
  values and, 14
Deming, W. Edwards, 167
Deployment
  daily, 68–69, 143
  incremental approach to, 62–63
  incremental design and, 109
  metrics for defects after, 79
Design. *See also* Incremental design
  Alexander's principles, 162
  common language for decision
    making, 172
  database design strategy, 107–108,
    172
  patterns and, 108, 173
  small scale, 171
Developers. *See* Programmers
Development. *See* Software
  development
Disney, 163
Diversity principle, 29
Documentation
  code and tests as basis of, 66
  communication and, 146
  "Rosetta Stone" document,
    114–115
  technical publications, 80–81
  of tests, 26
  Unified Process document driven
    basis, 169
Double-checking, defect testing,
  98–100
Drawings. *See* Images
Drawings, as communication
  medium, 174

DSDM (Dynamic Systems Develop-
  ment Method), 170
Dynamic Systems Development
  Method (DSDM), 170

E
Eclipse project, xv–xvi
Economics
  principles in XP, 25
  quality and, 33
Ego, thinking and, 165
Emergent processes, bibliographic
  references, 163–164
Emotions, fear as barrier to performance, 167
Employees. *See* Staffing
Energized work
  map of, 58
  as primary practice, 41–42
Ernst, Michael, 51, 173
Estimation
  benefit of early estimation, 44–45
  creating believable estimates,
    127–128
  planning and, 92, 93–94
  real time estimates, 168
  values and, 14
Execution, separating from planning
  in social engineering, 132
Executive, as team role, 78–79
Executive sponsorship
  crucial to success of XP, 90,
    119–121
  finding, 140
Expenses. *See* Costs
Experience, design process and, 107
"An Experimental Evaluation of
  Continuous Testing During
  Development" (Saff and Ernst),
  51, 173

F

Facilities. *See* Workspace
Failure
    dealing with consequences of,
        116–117
    learning from, 143
    as principle in XP, 32
Features
    customer control of, 128
    tracking projects by, 169
Feedback
    from continuous testing, 173
    Eclipse project and, xv
    finding defects and, 99
    measuring software projects, 169
    pay-per-use, 69–70
    reflection combined with doing,
        30
    types of, 20
    as value guiding development,
        19–20
Flow
    principles in XP, 30
    team approach and, 73–74
The Forest People (Turnbull), 4
Fowler, Martin, 95, 126
Fractals, 27

G

Gamma, Erich, 51
Gannt, Henry, 131
Gilbreth, Frank, 131
Gilbreth, Lillian, 131
Gladwell, Malcolm, 39
Global software development, 151
Goals
    executive role and, 78
    planning and, 91
    XP goals for software develop-
        ment, xxi

Graphics. *See* Images
Group dynamics, 143
Growth, as human need, 24

H

Health, pair programming and, 43
Hendrickson, Chet, 128
High-cost base areas, compared with
    low-cost base areas, 150
Hiring, 81–82
History, practice of, 167
Hopelessness, overcoming, 163
How Buildings Learn (Brand), 104
Human resources, reviews and hir-
    ing, 81–82
Humanity
    fear as barrier to performance, 167
    principle in XP, 24–25
    Sit Together practice and, 38
    workspace and, 40
Hunt, Andy, 140
Hygiene, 43

I

Illnesses. *See* Sicknesses
Images
    communicating with drawings,
        174
    communicating with graphs and
        pictures, 174
Improvement
    executive role and, 78
    noncontinuous nature of, 142
    principles in XP, 28
Incremental deployment, 62–63,
    169
Incremental design, 103–110
    daily focus of, 103
    database design strategy, 107–108
    deciding when to design, 105–107

Incremental design, *continued*
  Eclipse project and, xvi
  improvement as focus of, 28
  investing in, 172
  Once and Only Once heuristic,
    108
  as primary practice, 51–53
  simplicity of design, 109–110
  Smalltalk project, 127
  timing of design decisions, 109
  weakness of physical-based meta-
    phors for, 103–104
Industrial engineering, 131
Informative workplace, 39–41
  charts, 41
  human needs and, 40–41
  story cards, 40
Insight, 41
Integration, continuous integration
    practice, 49–50
Integrity, 159
Interaction designers, as team role,
    75
Investments
  measuring investment-to-return,
    79
  XP as expense or investment, 113
Iterations
  feedback cycles and, 7, 94
  planning frequency of, 121
  removing constraints or limita-
    tions, 168
  story implementation and, 127

J
JAD (Joint Application Develop-
    ment), 171
Jeffries, Ron, 126
Jensen, Brad, 119–121
Jobs, offshore development and,
    150

Joint Application Development
    (JAD), 171
Judgement, communication and,
    168
JUnit, xiv, 171, 173
Just In Time Software process,
    xiii–xiv

L
Leadership, 143
Learning
  applying new skills, 141
  conflict and disagreement and, 158
  by example, 143
  from failures, 32, 143
  reflection as basis of, 30
Life cycle models, 116
Listening skill
  community and, 157
  listening to feedback, 80, 141
  planning and, 93
Load tests, 101
Low-cost base areas, compared with
    high-cost base areas, 150

M
Maintenance
  applying XP to, 170
  project management and, 170
Management
  executives, 78–79
  product managers, 78
  project managers, 76–77, 92,
    113–114
  Scientific Management and, 131
  self-organizing systems as meta-
    phor for management, 164
Manual testing, 101
Manuals, 80–81. *See also*
    Documentation
Margins, in software development,
    165

Mathematics, programming as, 172
McConnell, Steve, 104–105, 173
Meetings, weekly cycles, 46
Metaphors
    chosen by interaction designers, 75
    code names and, 26
    driving XP, 12
    physical-based impose limits on
        software development, 104
    Scientific Management, 131
    self-organizing systems as meta-
        phor for management, 164
    thinking and, 162
    Unified Process emphasis on, 170
Metrics
    awareness and, 56
    feedback and, 169
    graphing, 174
    for health of XP team, 79
    measuring progress with tests, 102
    for XP, 145
Micro-optimization, 88
Mistakes. *See* Failure
Modernism, 161
Money. *See also* Costs
    pay-per-use and, 69–70
    time value of, 25
The Mountain People (Turnbull), 4
Multi-site development, 149–152
    global software development, 151
    high-cost base areas compared
        with low-cost base areas, 150
    practices and, 150
    principles and, 150
    reasons for, 149
    values and, 149
Mutual benefit, as principle in XP, 26

N
Names, coding style and, 26
Negotiated scope contract, 69

O
Offshore development. *See* Multi-site
    development
Ohno, Taiichi, 136, 174
Once and Only Once, heuristic for
    incremental design, 108
Online communities, XP, 158
Opportunity, as principle in XP,
    30–31
Option value, of systems and teams,
    25
Organizations
    reducing team sizes, 150
    reverting to old habits, 140
    scaling XP and, 113–114
Overall throughput, vs. micro-opti-
    mization, 88
Overproduction, as waste, 136
Overwork, holding back effort
    through, 6
Ownership, collective, 66. *See also*
    Responsibility

P
Pain, as factor in quick change, 142
Pair programming
    benefits of, 42–43
    continuous integration and, 50
    personal space and, 43–44
    as primary practice, 42–43
    reasons for applying, 35
    teamwork and, 66
    technical collaboration and, 57
    XP building on, xiv
Paradigms, 166
Partitioning systems
    architect's responsibility for, 76
    scaling XP and, 112
Patterns
    design process and, 108, 173
    XP and, xiv

Pay-per-release, 70
Pay-per-use, 69–70
People
    bibliographic references, 165–168
    change and, 155
    communication between business
        and technical people, 172
    as component of problems, 38
    scaling XP and, 111–112
Perfection, 28
Performance, fear as barrier to, 167
Performance tuning, 93, 125
Permaculture, 103, 162
Personal space, 43–44
Philosophy
    bibliographic references, 161–162
    of XP, 123
Physical environment. *See* Workspace
Planning, 91–95
    Chrysler Smalltalk project, 127
    deciding what to change first, 56
    estimation and, 92, 93–95
    goals and, 91
    incremental, xvi
    project managers responsibility for,
        77
    quarterly cycles and, 47–48
    scope as basis of, 92
    separating from execution in
        Taylorism, 132
    team cooperation in, 93
    technical details of, 168
    timescales and, 92–93
    weekly cycles and, 46–47
Politics, of offshore development,
    150
Postmodernism, 161
Practices
    based on values, 14
    compared with values, 14–15
    defined, 13

implementing primary before
    corollary, 61
ineffectiveness of dictating, 57
learning by example, 143
mapping, 58–59
multi-site development and, 150
overview of, 35–36
social relationships and, 154
win-win-win, 26
Practices, corollary, 61–73
    code and tests, 66–67
    customer involvement, 61–62
    daily deployment, 68–69
    incremental deployment, 62–63
    negotiated scope contract, 69
    pay-per-use, 69–70
    root cause analysis, 64–66
    shared code, 66
    shrinking teams, 64
    single code base, 67–68
    team continuity, 63–64
Practices, primary, 37–54
    continuous integration, 49–50
    energized work, 41–42
    incremental design, 51–53
    informative workplace, 39–41
    pair programming, 42–43
    quarterly cycles, 47–48
    sit together, 37–38
    slack, 48
    stories, 44–45
    ten-minute build, 49
    test-first programming, 50–51
    weekly cycles, 46–47
    whole team approach, 38–39
Predictability, as value, 22
Principles, 23–36
    baby steps, 33
    defined, 15
    diversity, 29
    economics, 25

failure, 32
flow, 30
humanity, 24–25
improvement, 28
learning by example, 143
multi-site development and, 150
mutual benefit, 26
opportunity, 30–31
overview of, 23
quality, 32–33
redundancy, 31–32
reflection, 29–30
responsibility, 34
self-similarity, 27–28
social relationships and, 154
Priorities, 109
aligning, 55–57
business, 67
economics of, 25
funding, 129
implementing highest priority first, 7–8
product managers and, 77
Problems
complexity in scaling XP, 115
as opportunity for change, 30–31
people-oriented solutions, 38
resolving in flow-based environment, 30
steps for working with big, 112
Product development, 170
Product managers, 77–78
Productivity
Energized Work principle and, 41
Scientific Management and, 131
TPS, 136
Programmers
global demand, 151
sharing responsibility with business interests, 155
as team role, 81

tests, 100
working with sponsors and users, 154
Programming
art of writing, 166
balancing human interests, 153–155
bibliographic references, 171–174
continuous integration practice, 49–50
pair programming principle, 42–43
for and by people, 168
pragmatic programmers, 140
short-cycle, 169
social and technical networks, 164
test-first programming, 50–51, 141, 143
Project management
bibliographic references, 168–171
Taylorist perspective, 170
Project managers
presenting information to organizations, 113–114
story cards and, 95
as team role, 76–77
Projects
cancellations, 5
feedback and, 169
tracking projects by features, 169
trouble indicators, 126
Pull, model of development, 87–88
Push, model of development, 87–88

Q

Quality
principles in XP, 32–33
project management and, 92
quality control in Deming's model, 167
social engineering and, 132–133
variable in zero-sum model, 161–162

Quality-of-life, 22
Quarterly cycles, 47–48, 114

R
Redundancy principle, 31–32
Refactoring, xiv, xv, 172
Reflection principle, 29–30
Regression testing, 65
Relationships
  business relationships, 1
  community, 157
  fostering strong, 154
  improving, 146
  mutual benefit as basis of, 26
  relational skills of programmers,
    81
  separating intimate relationships
    from work setting, 43
  in societies of abundance and scar-
    city, 167
  undermined by misalignment of
    authority and responsibility,
    141
Release cycle, reducing, 6
Requirements
  gathering, 137
  misused terminology in develop-
    ment, 44
Resources, in societies of abundance
  and scarcity, 167
Respect
  multi-site development and, 149
  in Ohno's management approach,
    174
  as value guiding development, 21
Responsibility
  accepted, 4, 165
  vs. control by others, xxii
  misalignment undermines trust,
    141
  as principle in XP, 34

shared code and, 66
sharing between programmers and
  business interests, 155
Revenue, measuring investment-to-
  return, 79
Review, of human resources, 81–82
Rewards, as control mechanism, 166
Risk
  big deployments and, 63
  daily deployment and, 68
  economic, 26
  of error, 49
  of failure, leading to success, 32
  management, 73, 116, 169
  negotiated scope contract and, 69
  not asking others to take risks you
    are not willing to take, 141
  partitioning and, 112
  silence as sound of risk piling up,
    79
  XP addresses at all levels, 7
Risk, in development process, 5–6
Roles flexibility, in XP programming,
  82–83
Root cause analysis, 64–66
"Rosetta Stone" document, 114–115

S
Sabre Airline Solutions, 119–121
Sadalage, Pramod, 107
Safety
  human needs, 24
  Sit Together practice and, 38
  as value, 22
Saff, David, 51
Scaffolding, incremental deploy-
  ment, 63
Scaling XP, 111–117
  consequences of failure, 116–117
  investments, 113
  organization size, 113–114

overview of, 111
people, 111–112
problem complexity and, 115
solution complexity and, 115–116
time, 114–115
Schedules, slipping, 5
Scientific Management, 131–132, 174
Scope
   business concerns dominating, 154
   as control mechanism, 33
   ongoing negotiation of, 69
   planning as means of managing, 92
   variable in zero-sum model, 161–162
Scope creep, 50
Seasons, as organizational timescale, 47
Security
   certifiable, 116–117
   as value, 22
Self-organizing systems, 164
Self-similarity principle, 27–28
Sexuality, in work environment, 43
Shape, self-similarity principle, 27
Shared code, 66
Shrinking teams, 64
Sicknesses, 41
Simplicity
   bibliographic reference, 161
   courage and, 21
   dealing with excess complexity, 115–116
   feedback and, 20
   incremental design, 109–110
   multi-site development and, 149
   as value guiding development, 18–19
Single code base, 67–68, 150
Sit together as a practice, 37–38, 145
Skiing, 165

Skills, learning and applying, 141
Slack, as primary practice, 48
Social change, 1
Social engineering, 132–133
Social relationships
   stratification lacking in TPS, 136
   XP applied in context of, 139
Software development
   advantages of XP for, 3–4
   community for, 157–160
   costs, 173
   cycles, xvi
   driving with stories, 169
   DSDM approach to rapid development, 170
   electrical engineering paradigm, 169
   global, 151
   goals of XP and, xxi
   limitations of Taylor's model when applied to, 132
   low-cost base areas vs. high-cost base areas, 150
   margins in, 165
   overproduction, 136–137
   push model contrasted with pull model, 87–88
   risk in, 5–6
   shortcomings of Taylorist approach, 166
   team-driven process, 12
   Theory of Constraints and, 168
   utility vs. technical virtuosity, 154
   values guiding, 18
Software engineering, 49
Solution complexity, 115–116
Sponsors
   executive sponsorship, 90, 119–121, 140
   working with developers and users, 154

Staffing
  managing turnover, 6
  scaling, 112
  needs of good developers, 24
  worker responsibility in TPS, 135–136
Static verification, 101
Stories
  breaking into tasks, 47
  deciding what to change first, 56
  driving development from, 169
  interaction designers writing, 75
  planning and, 91, 93–95
  as primary practice, 44–45
  product managers writing, 77–78
  project completion time and, 127
  slack time and, 48
  weekly cycles and, 46
Story cards
  example, 45
  in informative workplace, 40
  in planning process, 96
  presenting information to organizations, 113–114
Stress tests, 101
Subscription model, software marketing, 70
Success
  as goal, 146
  XP and, 4
Survival, problem solving and, 31
Systems
  bibliographic references, 164–165
  self-organizing, 164

T
Talking skills, 157
Tasks, breaking stories into, 47
Taylor, Frederick, 131–133, 150, 165, 167, 170

TDD (Test-Driven Development), 171
Team. *See also* Whole team practice
  approach to coding style, 17
  balancing individual needs with team needs, 24
  certification and accreditation, 146
  common factors in good software development teams, xxi–xxii
  communication as basis of cooperation, 18
  continuity, 63–64
  Disney's, 163
  diversity, 29
  models, 66
  orientation in XP, 6
  reducing size (shrinking) of, 64
  respect as key value to working of, 21
  reverting to old habits, 140
  scaling XP and, 112
  sexuality complicating working of, 43
  sharing power, 155
  size thresholds, 39
  software development as team-driven process, 12
  things that can go wrong, 168
  undermined by misalignment of authority and responsibility, 141
Team continuity, 63–64
Teamwork models, 66
Technical aspects
  communication between business and technical people, 172
  excellence in, 4
  technical fixes must be complemented by people-oriented solutions, 38

Technical collaboration, 57
Technical employment, 150
Technical publications, 80–81
Technical writers, as team role, 80–81
Technique, as basis of practices, 13
Ten-minute build, as primary practice, 49
Test-Driven Development (TDD), 171
Test-first programming, 50–51, 141, 143, 171
Testers, as team role, 74–75
Tests, 97–102
  automating, 100–101
  code and test cycle, 66–67, 101–102
  DCI, 98–99
  defect rates, 5
  defect reduction, 97–98
  documenting, 26
  double-checking, 100
  early and often, xvi
  feedback from continuous testing, 173
  frequency of, 100
  JUnit, 171
  learning from failures, 32
  measuring progress with, 102
  regression testing, 65
  static verification, 101
  system architecture, 75–76
  ten-minute build, 49
  test-first programming, 50–51, 141, 143
  unit tests, 173
  weekly cycles and, 46, 74
Theory of Constraints, 85–90
  bottlenecks and, 85–86
  identifying constraints, 86–87
  overall throughput vs. micro-optimization, 88
  push model of development contrasted with pull model, 87–88
  software development and, 168
  statement of theory, 86
  understanding systems, 164
  XP shifting constraints to non-software development areas, 89–90
Thinking
  ego and, 165
  linear vs. nonlinear, 174
  metaphors and, 162
Thomas, Dave, 140
ThoughtWorks, 107
Throughput, 88, 164
Time
  long-running projects and, 114–115
  planning and, 92–93
  project management and, 92
  quarterly cycles and, 47–48
  seasons and, 47
  time value of money, 25
  variable in zero-sum model, 161–162
  weekly cycles and, 46
The Tipping Point (Gladwell), 39
Toyota Production System (Ohno), 137
Toyota Production System (TPS), 135–138
  parallels to software development, 136–137
  production process, 136
  social stratification lacking in, 136
  waste reduced, 135–136
  worker responsibility in, 135–136
Tracking, projects by features, 169

Trust
    defects and, 97–98
    undermined by misalignment of
        responsibility, 141
Turnbull, Colin, 4

U

Underwork, holding back effort
    through, 6
Unit tests, xiv, xv, 173
UP (Unified Process), 170
User-interface design, 166
Users. *See also* Customers
    as team role, 81
    technical writers and, 80
Users, *continued*
    tests based on perspective of, 102
    working with developers and spon-
        sors, 154

V

Values, 17–22
    based on what really matters, 17
    change and, 56
    communication, 18
    compared with practices, 14–15
    courage, 20–21
    defined, 14
    feedback, 19–20
    guiding development, 18
    improvement and, 142
    integrity and, 159
    learning by example, 143
    multi-site development and, 149
    not using XP when organization
        values at odds with XP values,
        144
    other important, 22
    respect, 21
    simplicity, 18–19

W

Wabi-Sabi, 161
Waste
    customer involvement in reduc-
        ing, 61
    eliminating, 28
    overcommitment and, 48
    overproduction and, 136–137
    planning as necessary waste, 46–47
    redundancy and, 32
    Toyota success in eliminating,
        135–136
Waterfall process, 87, 146
Weekly cycles, 46–47, 74
Whole team practice, 73–83
    architects, 75–76
    customers, 61–62
    executives, 78–79
    failure to work together,
        73–74
    human resources, 81–82
    interaction designers, 75
    overview of, 38–39
    product managers, 77–78
    programmers, 81
    project managers, 76–77
    role flexibility and, 82–83
    technical writers, 80–81
    testers, 74–75
    users, 81
Win-win-win practices, 26
Work hours
    balancing with other human needs,
        24
    energized work principle and, 41
Workspace
    design of, 163–164
    informative workspace practice,
        39–41
    sit together practice, 38

X

XP, applying, 139–144
  coach selection, 143–144
  executive sponsorship, 119–121,
    140
  improvements, 142
  learning and applying skills, 141
  organization reverting to old hab-
    its, ways of doing things, 140
  social relationships and, 139
  staring with yourself, 140–141
  when not to apply XP, 144
XP, getting started, 55–59
  awareness of need for change,
    56–57
  change starts with yourself, 57
  changing one thing at a time, 55
  deciding what to change first, 56
  mapping practices and, 58–59

XP, overview
  aspects of, 2
  benefits of, 3
  business relationships and, 1
  certification and accreditation,
    146–147
  constraints shifted to non-
    software development areas,
    89–90
  defined, iv, 6–7
  distinguishing characteristics, 2
  metrics for, 145–146
  risk in development process and,
    5–6
  social change and, 1
  success and, 4

Z

Zero-sum model, 161–162

Note on Style

This book follows punctuation and grammar style as described in the *MLA Style Manual and Guide to Scholarly Publishing*, specifically with regard to comma and semicolon usage.

informIT